the
WARRIOR'S
ADVANCE

the
WARRIOR'S
ADVANCE

Learning to Stand, Walk, and War

from the Book of Ephesians

AWAKENED. *Born for the Battle*
DELIVERED. *Rescued, Redeemed, Restored*
VICTORIOUS. *Seated with Christ*
AUTHORIZED. *Power and Purpose*
NEW. *Calling Out the Warrior*
COURAGEOUS. *Walking in the Spirit*
EQUIPPED. *Ready for My Mission*

BY DOUG SMITH

By Doug Smith
© 2019 by Doug Smith

Cover design and Typesetting: Thinkpen Design

ISBN: 978-0-9986170-7-7

Visit the author's website at https://www.thewarriorsadvance.com/

CONTENTS

PRELUDE TO WAR

*Teach me how to live, O LORD. Lead me along the
right path, for my enemies are waiting for me.*

PSALM 27:11 NLT

*"The gateway to life is very narrow and the road
is difficult, and only a few ever find it."*

MATTHEW 7:14 NLT

In the summer of 2012, I rediscovered the ancient path. It was the same path I had excitedly ventured forth on sixteen years earlier—a path well journeyed by God's faithful in the Old Testament, blazed anew by Jesus' followers after His resurrection, and traveled by countless passionate believers over the past two thousand years. It's a path where calling meets destiny for those who hear the Voice behind them saying, "This is the way, walk in it" (Isaiah 30:21).

As for my journey on the path, after a few years of trekking through the wilderness, I had found a comfortable spot, set up camp—and stayed put. I settled—and why not? I was enjoying my new life in Christ with my beautiful wife and daughter. God had blessed me with a nice home and a pretty good paycheck. I went to church on Sundays and even answered the call to become a worship leader. But *something* was missing.

Gazing down that ancient path, I realized why I had abandoned it in the first place. It looked extremely unpredictable, challenging, and demanding. But—*yet*—it was beckoning me to step away from my comfortable, predictable life and move ahead into new frontiers. The promise of adventure and battle lay dead ahead, and the mere thought of advancing on the path made my spirit spring to life. Allowing the Spirit to lead me once again into the unknown felt primal and dangerous. God was stirring my heart and drawing me back to the narrow passageway—to the path of the warrior.

Only a true warrior—only *God's* warrior walking in *His* power—can navigate this path well. *Could I?* It's not for the faint of heart, the casual believer, or the Sunday morning Christian. No, this path is for the intrepid Christ-following soldier who recognizes the spiritual battle between God's kingdom of light and the dark evil of this world. This path is for the soldier who knows that, in God's strength, he must fight the battle daily for the good of his family and friends. He realizes that his strength, his faith, and his prayers are vital in helping those he loves travel this path alongside him.

If you're like me, you may consider yourself an unlikely warrior, and that is God's design. His army is void of the proud and arrogant. God is looking for the humble, obedient, and surrendered recruit whom He can train for war.

Venturing onto this path will cost us, challenge us, grow us, and bless us. For this path is narrow and the way, difficult. We will encounter many evil and cruel adversaries along the way, but this is our true destiny; this is the ancient way blazed by the Ancient of Days. He promises that His glorious presence will go before us, live inside us, and be our rear guard as we follow in His footsteps (Isaiah 52:12). Our holy and almighty God will lead us safely on, moment by moment, into the glorious and eternal plan He has for us.

So we stand at the trailhead together, sensing that this journey will change and enrich our lives in ways we can't even imagine. When we take the risk and step on to the path, the transformation begins: we will become more and more like our King. Healing and deliverance from fear await those who will—trusting in Him—forge ahead on this trail. Those of us willing to abandon our comfort zone and walk in our God-given authority will find adventure and victory. New and vital connections with fellow warriors await, relationships that will strengthen, encourage, and sharpen us as we journey on. Finally, a greater, more intimate and life-giving communion with the King is a blessing reserved for the disciplined and skilled warrior whom the Lord has equipped for the battle.

We can be sure this path will stretch us and test our faith, but those fires will also refine us and give us skills we need as God's soldiers. Our Commander wants us to choose to put everything on the line and put ourselves in the line of fire. He wants us to choose to be His warriors. But what need would there be for warriors if there is no war?

There *is* war. There *is* adventure.

Does that stir something inside of you?

The path is calling.

I

AWAKENED
BORN FOR THE BATTLE

THE WAR

Wake up, O sleeper, rise from the dead,
And Christ will shine on you.
EPHESIANS 5:14

"Why don't you come to Boot Camp?"

I'm sure I looked awkward as I fumbled for a reply.

"Really," he continued. "You should come to the Wild at Heart Boot Camp in August." Those words, from a man I had just met, would forever change my life and my walk with God....

As we talked, I realized that this man was asking me to take a huge leap out of my comfort zone and go to a men's conference, over a thousand miles from home, and spend four days with four hundred strangers—by myself. Would God really expect me to do something that far out of the box? I'm sure you know the answer, but I needed more convincing.

I wouldn't even have talked to Allen Arnold that sunny day in June if the Holy Spirit hadn't prompted me to go to the morning's chapel service. The company I worked for had a service every Friday, and each week a different employee would give a devotional talk for fifteen minutes or so. The site of those meetings would alternate weeks, one week being at the corporate building and the next, at the distribution center where I worked. I heard some great devotions over the years, but I rarely went to the corporate service. I knew, though, that on this particular Friday, Allen was speaking, and I had heard that he was about to leave our company, move to Colorado, and go to work for John Eldredge, one of my favorite authors. So I felt compelled to attend.

As it turned out, that Friday was Allen's last day with the company, and he delivered a great message about how our lives are epic stories to be walked out with God daily. His talk was all the more poignant in light of the fact that he was about to take a big step of faith. At the end of the service, I approached him and said I admired him for stepping out and making the move to Colorado to work with John. And that's when he said, "You should come to the Wild at Heart Boot Camp in August." Allen went on to say the lottery for the event would open up in a couple weeks if I were interested. I gave my usual safe answer: "I'll pray about it." Then I wished Allen all the best and went on my way.

Over the next few days, I tried to let go of any thoughts about Boot Camp, but the Spirit kept whispering, "Don't dismiss this." It wasn't long after my brief conversation with Allen that I was on the Ransomed Heart website checking out exactly what Boot Camp entailed. I remember being filled with both excitement and apprehension. So many men sign up for these events that the attendees are chosen by lottery, so I said a prayer, entered my name, and waited to see if my attending would get a "go" from God.

A week later I opened my inbox and saw the email from Ransomed Heart. Excitedly, I clicked on it and read, "You have been selected for Boot Camp." I found out later that over a thousand men had applied; I was one of the chosen four hundred. The stage was set, and the journey would soon begin.

THE AWAKENING

So on a hot day in August 2012, I boarded a plane for Denver out of Nashville. From there, I hopped on a bus for an incredible two-hour

ascent into the Rocky Mountains. Finally, we arrived at this amazing
compound nestled in the heart of the Rockies. After dinner, we sat
down in a beautiful, rustic theater for our first session. My heart was
ready. The lights dimmed, and we watched an intense battle scene from
the movie *Act of Valor*. Then, the mood now set, John Eldredge walked
up on the stage, and a Scripture verse flashed across the huge screen as
he spoke. It was my verse—the one the Lord had been whispering in
my ear for quite some time:

> The LORD is a warrior. The LORD is His name.
> (Exodus 15:3 NIV)

I knew, in my heart, that I was right where God wanted me.

John began to expound on the fact that since the Lord is a warrior
and we are made in His image, we must be warriors too. To be honest,
I didn't feel like a warrior in any sense of the word. Accepting John's
statement was quite a stretch for me. In fact, I felt more like a casualty
of war. But that night my heart came alive, and I was fully engaged in
what John was saying. On that cool evening in the Colorado Rockies,
the truth that I am a soldier in Christ's army and I have what it takes to
live a victorious Christian life was starting to set me free. The warrior
within was starting to awaken.

Throughout the weekend we had "covenant of silence" time after
certain sessions: all four hundred of us would silently file out of the
theater to spend time alone with God. I would find a place with a view
of the breathtaking mountains and sit there quietly and pray. I was
desperate to hear God's voice. Although men were all around me, no
one said a word. They, too, wanted to hear from God. It was as if we
were on holy ground. Each time I bowed my head, I heard the Lord
whisper the same words: "Wake up, Doug. I have a plan for your life,
and there are people who need you."

Transformation took place that weekend in the Rockies. My face
wasn't glowing like Moses' when I descended the mountain and returned

to Tennessee, but a new spark had been ignited in me. I prayed that the Lord would protect it and fan it into flame. I thought about Boot Camp nearly every day, months after my mountaintop experience. I listened to the songs we had sung in worship, I thought about the powerful words that had been breathed into my soul, and I searched the Scriptures daily for answers to my many questions. I realized that a lot of the things I believed about life—and about myself—were simply lies I had swallowed. I was beginning to understand just how wounded I really was—and how badly I wanted to be healed.

Everything about my spiritual life changed after Colorado. I began poring over the Scriptures to learn all I could about the Enemy and this spiritual war the conference speakers had talked about so much. I began to understand that when fear tried to overwhelm me, the Enemy was fueling that fear, and I don't have to just put up with it. I started realizing that when my wife and I got really out of sync, the Evil One was lurking in the shadows trying to divide us and conquer us. But more than anything, I could feel Jesus encouraging me, whispering in my ear, "You are a warrior, and I am with you always." I had a new sense of peace that I hadn't felt since giving my heart to Christ fifteen years earlier. I was starting to advance, and God was opening my eyes to see a whole new world.

An invisible world.

THE INVISIBLE REALM

God created everything in the heavenly realms and on earth.
He made the things we can see and the things we can't see—such
as thrones, kingdoms, rulers, and authorities in the unseen world.
COLOSSIANS 1:16 NLT

I guess I have always kind of glossed over verses like the one above. *There are kingdoms and rulers in an unseen world—really?* It sounds so Star Trek-ish! But the Bible teaches that there is not only the physical world where we reside, but also the spiritual world, invisible to us, but very real. These two worlds not only exist simultaneously, but one is always affecting the other whether we acknowledge that fact or not. A lot of what we experience in our physical world has a spiritual counterpart in what Paul called "the heavenly realms." This is reality in the kingdom of God, and, as Christian warriors, it's our duty to understand how this unseen world can affect our daily lives. Such knowledge isn't reserved solely for ministers or super-spiritual Christians; this is basic training that every warrior in the Lord's army should have. But most of us don't—and Satan makes sure of that. Colossians 1:16, however, confirms that this realm exists with its own thrones, kingdoms, rulers, and authorities: it is the invisible world of the Godhead, the angel armies, Satan, and his minions.

Even though I had been a Christian for many years, I hadn't given this realm much thought, and I had no idea of the important role that angels play in God's story—and ours. So let's explore their world for a few moments. Where did the angels come from, and how can they affect our lives?

ANGEL ARMIES

The verses below tell us God created the angels as eternal beings, and they were all present when He created the earth:

Praise Him, all His angels; praise him, all His hosts!...Let them praise the name of the LORD, for He commanded and they were created. He also established them forever and ever. (Psalm 148:2, 5–6)

"Where were you when I laid the foundations of the earth?... When the morning stars sang together, and all the sons of God shouted for joy?" (Job 38:4, 7)

Multitudes of angels—the "morning stars" and "sons of God," in the Job passage—were on the scene praising God and celebrating as He created the earth. Revelation 5:11 says that worshipping around the throne of God are "ten thousand times ten thousand, and thousands of thousands." I know that isn't meant to be a mathematical equation, but this single verse points to over a hundred million angels! Hebrews says that in the city of the living God is "an innumerable company of angels" (Hebrews 12:22). The number of angels is truly mind-boggling!

So what roles do these angelic creatures play in God's kingdom? God's angel armies encamp around those who fear Him (Psalm 34:7); they worship God and live close to Him (Hebrews 1:6); and they are mighty in battle. A lone angel killed 185,000 Assyrians in a single night (2 Kings 19:35–36). All angels serve under the authority of Christ (1 Peter 3:21–22; Colossians 1:16). When Christ comes back, the angels will gather those who are saved (Matthew 24:30–31) and cast the unsaved into the furnace of fire (Matthew 13:41–42). Angels patrol the earth (Zechariah 1:10–17), and although they have spiritual bodies, they can appear on Earth in physical form when God allows it (Judges 6:12; Luke 1:11). Psalm 103 gives us more great insight into the purpose and mission of the angels:

Bless the LORD, you his angels, who excel in strength, who do His word, heeding the voice of His word. Bless the LORD, all you His hosts, you ministers of His, who do His pleasure. (Psalm 103:20–21)

We can see here that angels were created to worship God, they have supernatural strength, and they listen to God's commands as He instructs them how to minister to us. The word *minister* means "to attend or serve."[1] As the writer of Hebrews says, "Are [God's angels] not all ministering spirits sent forth to minister for those who will inherit salvation?" (Hebrews 1:14).

So let's look at a few examples of angels ministering to people. In Genesis 22, an angel called out to Abraham from heaven to stop him from sacrificing Isaac, the son he had waited, literally, a hundred years to have. In Luke 4, angels ministered to Jesus after His intense battle with Satan in the wilderness. Also, in the book of Acts, an angel freed Peter from prison not just once, but on two different occasions (Acts 5:19; 12:3–19). How incredible is that! Angel-perpetrated jailbreaks! Acts 12:5 tells us exactly why the angels were dispatched on Peter's behalf: "Peter was therefore kept in prison, but constant prayer was offered to God for him by the church." That is the secret: prayer puts angels in motion—and demons to flight.

OPEN THE EYES OF MY HEART

In 2 Kings 6, we get a fascinating glimpse into the invisible world of the angel armies. A great Syrian battalion was bearing down on Elisha to capture him. When Elisha's servant saw the massive army with horses and chariots surrounding them, he asked Elisha, "What shall we do?" Elisha answered:

> Do not fear, for those who are with us are more than those who are with them. (2 Kings 6:16)

Then Elisha prayed and asked God to open his servant's eyes, and the Lord answered by opening up the invisible realm to him. The young servant then saw that all around them on the mountain were horses and chariots of fire. Angelic armies were on the scene prepared for battle. In this case, though, the faithful prophet asked God to strike his enemies with blindness, and the Lord did just that. How incredible to know that we can pray and ask God to not only remove our spiritual blindness, but also to deliver us in the spiritual battles we face.

Note: As we prepare to walk this path, I will point out some key battle strategies we will need for our journey. Here is the first one:

> **Battle Strategy**: When under spiritual attack, ask God to open your eyes and give you insight about how to pray against the Enemy's devices.

Another story I love is in 2 Samuel 5. David knew the Philistines had gathered against him, so he asked God, "Shall I go up against the Philistines?" The Lord replied: "You shall not go up, circle around behind them and come upon them in front of the mulberry trees. And it shall be, when you hear the sound of marching in the tops of the mulberry trees, then you shall advance quickly" (2 Samuel 5:23–24). How cool is that! God told David to not move until he heard the angel armies going ahead of him into the battle. This scene offers further confirmation that to gain victory here on Earth, we need intervention from the heavenly realms.

Joshua also had an incredible encounter with the spiritual realm before the battle of Jericho. Here, the pre-incarnate Christ appeared to Joshua and identified Himself as "the Commander of the army of the Lord" (Joshua 5:14). Not only that, but when Joshua first looked up, he saw that "the Man stood opposite him with His sword drawn in His hand" (v. 13). So why on earth would the Lord need a sword and an angel army unless a battle was raging? Answer: a battle *was* raging— and it continues today! A powerful force of evil is set against us, and it is led by a ruthless tyrant who truly is public enemy number one. So let's go on our own reconnaissance mission and gather some needed intel about our formidable and invisible Enemy.

KNOW YOUR ENEMY

No age needs the plain, unvarnished truth about [the Devil] more than this generation. We need the light of that

*truth as a warning, as an incentive to vigilance, and as
an inspiration to effort. We need the knowledge about the
Enemy—his character, presence, and power—in order to
rouse men to action. This knowledge is vital to victory.*

E. M. BOUNDS [2]

The first rule in any war is... know your enemy.

As time passed after Boot Camp, I realized more and more just how deep a sleep I had been lulled into. Over the years I'd read many verses about the devil, but somehow they just didn't seem to sink in. It's as if I kept hitting the spiritual snooze alarm and going back to sleep. I believed the Enemy existed, but, really, how much difference does he actually make in my life? This world is just screwed up. I just have a lot of personal problems. What does the devil have to do with any of it?

The more I woke up to spiritual realities and the more I learned about the Enemy, the more I understood why he had so successfully wreaked havoc in my life: I hadn't been trained to recognize his traps and tactics, so I was an easy target. I also realized—and was troubled by the fact—that most people aren't fond of talking about a believer's battle against Satan. But Jesus clearly told us that Satan is bent on stealing, killing, and destroying us (John 10:10). Even so, his name rarely came up in the churches I had attended. I would have thought that, after being a Christian for sixteen years, I would have heard someone—apart from the Bible and a few books I'd read—mention that we are engaged in massive warfare against a wicked and persistent foe. That would have been good information to know as I limped along in my Christian walk.

God, on the other hand, talks about the Evil One quite often in His Word. He discloses complete intelligence about our Enemy, describing him in different ways that reveal his wicked nature and intent. Scripture tells us, "Your adversary the devil walks about like a roaring lion, seeking whom he may devour" (1 Peter 5:8). *Devil* means "slanderer," and *Satan* means "adversary." So we can fully expect our

Enemy to try to slander and discredit us every chance he gets. As the tempter he will entice us to sin (Matthew 4:3). He is described as a "great dragon ... who deceives the whole world" (Revelation 12:9). And, Jesus said, our Enemy—in addition to being a murderer—is the father of lies (John 8:44) who accuses us before God day and night (Revelation 12:10). Paul described our Enemy as a master military tactician leading mighty demonic forces of evil (Ephesians 6:11–12). Still, Satan is rarely the topic of conversation or the Sunday sermon. Why? I'll tell you why: because that's part of his game. He makes everything and everyone—including you and me—appear to be the problem. After all, the devil is just a myth, a little red creature with pointy ears and a pitchfork, right?

Credit Jesus with giving Satan the lofty title "father of lies" (John 8:44 NIV). Jesus told us straight up, "When [Satan] speaks a lie, he speaks from his own resources" and "There is no truth in him" (v. 44). So we know that Satan is constantly speaking lies, but are we recognizing his voice? If we don't—and if we take his bait and believe the lie—we give him a foothold, and footholds lead to strongholds. A *stronghold* is a place of personal bondage built on a lie or point of deception that the Enemy has been able to establish in our minds because we either didn't know or haven't trusted God's truth. Satan then speaks that lie over and over like a broken record. You know the voice. We all do: *You are worthless. You will never amount to anything. You are so stupid.... You don't fit in....* or (my personal favorite) *You will never change.* Knowing human nature and our weaknesses, Satan finds a lie we are apt to believe. If and when we come into agreement with it, he ensnares us. He then just feeds the lie and fortifies the stronghold day after day.

Clearly, this spiritual battle against the Evil One is fought in our minds. Your mind is the battlefield, and whoever is winning on that front, controls the war. You can try all the positive thinking in the world, but it can never overcome the fortified strongholds once the Enemy has them in place. Only the Word of God proclaimed by a surrendered saint has the power to do that. I will talk more about strongholds and the lies we believe in later chapters, but for now, what are some other ways the Enemy can hinder God's people?

OPPOSING FORCES

Paul wrote to the church in Thessalonica and told them, "We wanted to come to you—even I Paul, time and again—but Satan hindered us" (1 Thessalonians 2:18). Really? Satan was blocking the missionary travels of the great apostle Paul? Who knew the Enemy could do that?

In another battle scene, Daniel had been fasting and praying for three weeks in response to a vision he'd had. Finally, an angel appeared and told him that the moment he had started praying, "Your words were heard; and I have come because of your words" (Daniel 10:12). The reason for the delay? The angel's arrival was slowed by a battle in the spiritual realm. The spirit prince of Persia, a territorial spirit in Satan's army, blocked God's messenger. The angel went on to tell Daniel that the archangel Michael had come to help him in the fight (v. 13). The fact that warfare in the heavens delayed Daniel's answer for three full weeks is proof positive that the war in heaven affects us directly and may even be delaying answers to our prayers.

In a battle scene from Jesus' life, the Lord told His disciples He must go to Jerusalem to suffer and die, but Peter stepped up and said, "This shall not happen to You!" (Matthew 16:22). The Lord replied, "Get behind Me, Satan! You are an offense to Me, for you are not mindful of the things of God, but the things of men" (v. 23). Wow! Satan had gotten inside Peter's head and convinced him to try to stop Jesus' journey to the cross. Incredible! In that moment, though, I'm sure Peter thought he was doing a brave and noble thing.

Just as Satan prompted Peter to discourage Jesus, the Enemy tried to incite Job's wife against him. At the beginning of the book of Job, Satan petitioned God on two different occasions for permission to attack Job, saying, "He will surely curse You to Your face!" (Job 2:5). After the attacks, Job was suffering mightily, and his wife said, "Do you still hold fast to your integrity? Curse God and die!" (v. 9). Now where do you suppose Job's wife got the notion to tempt him to do that?

If Satan could keep Paul from going to a church to minister, delay a response to Daniel's prayer, convince Peter to rise up against the Son of God, and use Job's own wife against him, do you think he could be using those tactics on us as well? When we try to pray but our minds are flooded with a million thoughts and distractions, do you think that at least some of that noise might be someone's design? Are our prayers being hindered? The book of James says, "The prayer of a righteous person has great power and produces wonderful results" (James 5:16 NLT). I think the Enemy tries everything he can to interfere with our prayer time and keep us from getting "wonderful results" that glorify God.

One day, my wife, Cindy, and I were having a little spat that started out as no big deal. I really don't even remember what it was about, but the longer it went on, the angrier I got. Negative words started flooding my mind. I absolutely knew the Holy Spirit wanted me to keep my mouth shut, but I couldn't stem the tide. As the words were flying out of my mouth, I knew—in my spirit—that I had taken the bait. Feelings were hurt. Tears flowed. Afterward, I felt like a complete failure as a husband. Even after I apologized to her and repented of my sin before God, the Enemy kept bombarding me with words of condemnation for my being so cruel. He had enticed me to do it, and then he condemned me after I did. The Evil One is relentless.

HE TRAINS MY HANDS FOR WAR

Strange as it may sound, knowing Peter took the bait and blew it actually encourages me. Maybe I'm not just a bad Christian or loser husband, which is what the Enemy loves to tell me when things like that happen. Maybe at times I have just been a pawn of the Evil One who entices me to do his dirty work when I let my guard down. I started learning that I could choose to not take the bait. I could choose to submit to

God and resist the Devil. I could choose to walk in the Spirit and, like Jesus did in Matthew 4:10, say, "Away with you, Satan! In Jesus' name I command you to leave!" and make my Enemy flee.

I also realized that it was time for me to clean off the hard drive, reboot the system, and renew my mind with God's Word. I had much to learn, but this time I would let God lead the way. My job was to trust Him, obey Him, and be an apprentice. *His* apprentice. I was a novice at best. I needed to become a student of the Master and learn the art of spiritual warfare. Only then could I make any real difference in this world and in this war being waged, and—trust me—war *is* being waged.

To be honest, the idea of spiritual warfare always sounded a little weird to me, so I just didn't pay it much attention. Now I realize how naïve that was. As I said, I knew the Enemy existed, but I had no idea how much he was adversely affecting my life. He hates me with cruel hatred, knows all my weaknesses, and loves to expose them every chance he gets. And because I was still nursing old wounds and the aftereffects of years of prodigal living, I was very vulnerable to every attack and lie he hurled my way. I fell for every trick in his book even long after I became a Christian.

This book, in some ways, is a chronicle of my awakening and uncovering of the truth about spiritual warfare and the God who leads our army. I am not a trained theologian; I'm just a guy learning to fight in this war one battle at a time. I don't know exactly what God has in store for me on this journey, but I do know I am a warrior in God's army who has the predestined purpose of advancing His kingdom on the Earth. I wouldn't have been able to say that with any confidence until my awakening at Boot Camp.

Then, driving home from work one afternoon, I felt the Lord say, "Your life is an invasion of Enemy territory." I had never thought of it that way, but the statement made perfect sense. Jesus called Satan "the ruler of this world" three times in the gospels (John 12:31, 14:30, 16:11). In addition, in the wilderness temptation, Satan said to Jesus, "All these [kingdoms of the world] I will give You if You fall down and worship me" (Matthew 4:9). Jesus didn't argue or try to correct him. Satan offered Jesus the whole world because it was his to offer: he took control when Adam fell. That is why the life of the Christian is so greatly opposed in this world: we are not welcome here where Satan presides.

The hard truth is, we have a formidable Enemy who rules the world system; his mission is to annihilate us or, at the very least, render us ineffective. He thrives on keeping us distracted, distressed, and disoriented. He will stop at nothing to make our lives miserable whether or not we acknowledge him as real and active in this world. Actually, he prefers not to be acknowledged. Then his work is much easier and so much more effective. But in order for us to really understand this battle and our role in it, we need to understand why we have an Enemy to begin with. How, exactly, did we inherit this war?

INSURRECTION

Once upon a time, in a kingdom not so far away, there lived a magnificent and powerful angel. He was incredibly beautiful, loved and respected by all, and exemplary in his love for and service of all those under his authority. Also a gifted and anointed worship leader, he led the choirs of heaven in joyous worship of the King. He served the King and the kingdom well—until he chose the path of iniquity. You see, over time, this angel became discontent about being second to the Great King. Committing high treason, he began plotting to overthrow the kingdom.

The beautiful angel's name was Lucifer, meaning "Light Bearer" (pretty ironic since he became the prince of darkness). Although the Bible doesn't say definitively, many of the church fathers believed the angel Lucifer to be the rebellious one who became our archenemy, Satan. Lucifer fell in love with his own beauty and, puffed up with pride and self-centeredness, proclaimed, "I will exalt my throne above the stars of God… I will be like the Most High" (Isaiah 14:13–14). Lucifer was tired of praising God and bowing down to Him. This angel wanted to be the focus of that kind of worship, so he rebelled, earning his new name of Satan (meaning "adversary") or the Devil.

Not satisfied to be alone in his rebellion, Satan recruited a mass army of angels and staged a revolt against God. War ensued in the third heaven, but Satan and his armies had no chance. Here is how it all went down as described in the book of Revelation:

> [Satan's] tail drew a third of the stars of heaven... War broke out in heaven: Michael and his angels fought with the dragon; and the dragon and his angels fought, but they did not prevail, nor was a place found for them in heaven any longer. So the great dragon was cast out, that serpent of old, called the Devil and Satan, who deceives the whole world; he was cast to the earth, and his angels were cast out with him. (Revelation 12:4, 7–9)

War broke out in heaven? I can't even imagine that scene. But we see in these verses just how bold, seductive, and persuasive Satan can be. He managed to convince one-third of all the angels (referred to as "the stars of heaven") that they could win a war against their own Creator, against God Almighty!

It appears that Satan and his minions rebelled and were cast out of heaven at some point after the seven days of creation, but before the events of Genesis 3 when he tempted Adam and Eve to rebel against God just as he had. On day six God had said everything was "very good" in the garden, and He "blessed the seventh day," so Satan couldn't have been on the scene yet (Genesis 1:31; 2:3). Interestingly enough, though, Satan (as Lucifer) seems to have been in the Garden of Eden before he fell into sin. Scholars believe that Ezekiel 28:13–15 not only refers to the king of Tyre, but also to Lucifer:

> "You were in Eden, the garden of God... You were the anointed cherub... You were perfect in your ways from the day you were created, till iniquity was found in you." (Ezekiel 28:13–15)

Both Isaiah 14 and Ezekiel 28 appear to describe Lucifer's great fall, from a beautiful creature of God into the mire of pride, rebellion, and sin. The next time Satan appears in Scripture, he is the devil-serpent in the Garden of Eden where he waged war against God's image bearers.

THE BATTLE FOR EARTH

In the Garden of Eden, Eve became humankind's first casualty of war when she fell prey to Satan's clever deception. His simple lie convinced her that God was holding out on her and that if she ate from the tree that God had forbidden, she "[would] be like God" (Genesis 3:5).

Though God was meeting her every need, Eve's lust for more power proved to be too much. Eve succumbed to the worldly temptations of lust, greed, and pride and partook of the fruit on the forbidden tree. Genesis 3:6 says, "[She] saw that the tree was good for food" (lust of the flesh); "that it was pleasant to the eyes" (lust of the eyes); "and a tree desirable to make one wise" (the pride of life). Even today, most of the temptations we face fall into one of these three categories—lust of the flesh, lust of the eyes, and pride of life (see 1 John 2:16).

Back to the Garden and what may be the saddest part of the story. God had commissioned Adam to be the guardian of Eden (Genesis 2:15), yet Adam stood there, passively, silently witnessing his wife's fall. Then he, too, ate the fruit, joining her in the rebellion against God that severed their intimate relationship with Him. The result: we lost Eden. More specifically, we lost our authority to rule over Satan. The Evil One's diabolical plan worked masterfully and, as a result, life on this planet would never be the same. Satan had declared war on God's people and had won the first battle.

Yet even after Adam and Eve both rebelled in the Garden, who did God go looking for? The man—Adam—who had retreated and gone into hiding. (Sound familiar?) God called out the same three words He is calling out to men today: "Where are you?" (Genesis 3:9). God had expected Adam to step up in obedience, fulfill his role as Eden's defender and Eve's protector, and take charge in the battle for the Garden and for his wife.

God expects the same from every one of His sons today. God has given each of us our own gardens to tend, so to speak. Our homes, our families, our workplaces—these are the domains that God has entrusted to us, and He expects us to protect and defend them by keeping the Enemy out. Hear this: God holds you responsible, as His warrior, to stand your ground against the Enemy and fight on behalf of your loved ones. When the lives of your family and friends are going down in flames, God is calling out, "Where are you?" He created you to be a warrior, and you are to act like a warrior. He created you to fight—so fight you must!

VICTORY AT CALVARY

What Adam lost in Eden, Jesus won back at Calvary. It was there that the war changed dramatically. On the cross, Jesus delivered a crushing blow to Satan, disarming him and stripping him of his authority over believers (Colossians 2:15). However, this is still Enemy-occupied territory, and Satan can wreak havoc in our lives if we don't understand our authority and our identity in Christ. Satan still "prowls around like a roaring lion" looking to devour us (1 Peter 5:8 NIV), but he can't attack believers beyond what God permits or we allow.

As an angel, Satan does wield great power, but his power is limited. He is no match for the God of all creation. Our God is omniscient (all knowing), omnipotent (all powerful), and omnipresent (always present everywhere). Satan is none of these so, for instance, he can't be in more than one place at a time. In *Overcoming the Enemy* Charles Stanley wrote this:

Many people believe they are doing constant battle with Satan. In all likelihood, they have never had a single battle with Satan himself. The forces they have battled are Satan's demons, the fallen angels who joined Lucifer in rebelling against God.[3]

I had never thought of it that way, but in most cases we are probably dealing with Satan's minions who have all the time in the world to try to trip us up. The gospels contain story after story of Jesus casting out these fallen spirits that were tempting and tormenting people. These agents of Satan haven't just gone away over time. They are still prowling, still looking for access points into our lives.

As for unbelievers, their situation is altogether different. Satan already rules their lives, yet most people are totally unaware of it. Satan likes it that way; ignorance about him enables him to keep people as his slaves. I think many nonbelievers believe, as I used to, that since they are not really hurting anyone as they live their lives, they're okay. If asked, they would say they stand on neutral ground spiritually, but the Bible declares there is no neutral ground: the whole world lies under the sway of the wicked one (1 John 5:19).

A WORLD IN NEED OF WARRIORS

That's why the need for spiritual warriors is so great. The Enemy has both darkened the minds of unbelievers and worked hard to convince the church that he is not the problem. So his work has gotten way too easy. The Bible clearly says in Ephesians 6:12 that our struggle is not against flesh and blood. My battle is not with my wife, or that family member, or the person who just offended me at church; my battle is against the spiritual forces of evil. So, as warriors walking in the Spirit, we are to ask Jesus to help us discern what is going on behind the scenes in every battle we face. He will help us sharpen our skills as He trains us to not react in the physical world until we discern what is going on in the spiritual realm behind it.

Spiritual war is a day-to-day reality for every Christian who professes Christ as their Savior. Jesus will one day return as our conquering King and send Satan and his armies to their ultimate punishment, but until that day the spiritual war rages on, and we are called to engage in it. Remember, though, we are never alone. Christ is with us, and His angel armies are always at the ready when we pray: He will command His angels concerning you to guard you in all your ways (Psalm 91:11 NIV).

Imagine this scene: you are in desperate trouble, something terrible has happened to you here on Earth, and you cry out to Jesus. Your prayer goes immediately before His throne, and He summons the angel He has hand-selected for the assignment. The angel enters the throne room, bows before the King, and says, "I am at Your service." The Commander gives Him full intel on the situation and then outlines the mission. The angel listens intently, knowing he is being entrusted with an honorable and important assignment. He is being commissioned by the King of kings to war for one of His adopted sons. The angel can't help himself. A huge grin comes over his face as he looks confidently at his King. The Commander returns his smile, nods, and simply says, "Go!"

THE WAR RAGES ON

The LORD is with you, mighty warrior.
JUDGES 6:12 NIV

From start to finish, the Bible is a book of love and war, beauty and battle. We talk a lot about God's love, as we should: He is a God of love to be sure. But I think we've somehow ignored the fact that God is also a warrior. When I started reading the Bible in light of that great truth, I was stunned to discover that war and war imagery are major components of the story God is telling. In the Old Testament, the word *sword* appears 357 times; *enemies*, 252 times; *war*, 216 times; and *battle*, 171 times. Why all the war speech? Because there *is* war—mostly physical battles in the Old Testament, more clearly spiritual in the New—and until we come to terms with that, we will never recognize, much less be victorious in the battles of life. Only with such victories will we know the real peace our Commander offers. Like it or not, we live in a war zone. An invisible, spiritual war is being waged against us, and the battle is for the eternal souls of men and women. I am not being overly dramatic when I say the lives of our spouses, children, family, and friends hang in the balance of this spiritual war. The Lord started asking me some tough questions: "Who will fight for them if you won't? Who will stand in the gap for them if you don't?" God was calling out the warrior in me.

The battle lines have been clearly drawn for what is definitely not your typical war. This war has eternal consequences: though it started way back in the Garden of Eden, we woke up to the same war this morning. Satan and his army haven't changed or altered their strategy much at all. Why would they? It's still working. They simply look for any possible means to accuse, deceive, slander, and destroy us. The more we know about how they operate, the better. Gaining this knowledge and being prepared for war will require time and training in God's Boot Camp. But this well-invested time and energy will result in transformation from old to new,

> from fear to faith,
> from lamb to lion,
> from weakness to warrior!

WAR ROOM DISCUSSION

1. The Lord God is a warrior (Exodus 15:3), you are made in His image (Genesis 1:26), so you must be a warrior as well. What does this truth mean to you today?

2. What wounds have you sustained along this journey of life and will now lay at Jesus' feet for Him to heal and redeem?

3. Which example of angels ministering to a person—Abraham, Jesus, Peter, Elisha, David, Joshua—do you find most encouraging? Why?

4. What paradigm shift came with the insight that your life is an invasion of Enemy territory?

5. Why is it essential to recognize that we live in a spiritual war zone and that we are battling spiritual forces of evil?

2

AWAKENED

BORN FOR THE BATTLE

THE WARRIOR

*Call out your best warriors. Let all your
fighting men advance for the attack.*

JOEL 3:9 NLT

"The Kingdom of Heaven has been forcefully advancing."

MATTHEW 11:12 NLT

ADVANCING THROUGH EPHESIANS

Nearly every day, even months after my Boot Camp experience, I was
still on the quest. I couldn't let it go. I dug deeper into the Bible and
started reading books on spiritual warfare and the Enemy's tactics. I
thought differently and prayed differently. I knew I would never be the
same. I also knew I needed to both understand the war and process the
carnage it had left behind in my life.

In the midst of all of this, God also began stirring in my heart the
desire to share this message and wake up other warriors. I started
talking to Darrell, a close friend of mine, about how I felt God was
calling me to put together a men's retreat that would focus on the
warrior path. The ironic part is, I am not big on public speaking,
and "warrior" is probably not a term most people would choose to

describe me. Nonetheless, I had an emerging desire to show others the path I had discovered, and I felt God strongly leading me in that direction.

Darrell sent me an email one day stating, "These conferences should be called *advances*, not *retreats*." *Brilliant!* I thought. I looked up the word *advance*, and the definitions were perfect: "to accelerate the growth or progress of: to raise to a higher rank: move forward."[1] Yes, that was it. This gathering was to be an advance!

A few days later, I felt the Lord saying that the word *advance* was an acrostic for the message He had for me to deliver. Within minutes, I had a particular word assigned to each letter:

AWAKENED

DELIVERED

VICTORIOUS

AUTHORIZED

NEW

COURAGEOUS

EQUIPPED

Shortly after that, I was reading the introduction pages to Ephesians in the *New Spirit-Filled Life Bible*, and the notes mentioned a progression in Ephesians that shows us how to stand, walk, and war. As I read through it, the Lord clearly showed me this evolutionary process of learning, first, to *stand* on the truth of who of we are in Christ (Ephesians 1–3), then to *walk* in the power of the Holy Spirit (Ephesians 4–6:9), and then to *war* in Christ's army with a greater understanding of the spiritual battle (Ephesians 6:10–24). Ephesians— from its first verse to its very last—reveals the warrior path like no other book in the Bible. For me, this discovery was revolutionary: I had found a timeless pathway for Christian living. I was beyond excited and ended up spending countless hours studying Ephesians over the ensuing months.

As if seeing the stand, walk, and war pattern weren't exciting enough, the Lord began to show me how this Ephesians process fit perfectly with the *ADVANCE* acrostic. Now I was totally convinced that God had given me both this message and this mission for my life in the coming season. But first I needed to live what I felt called to share: I needed to advance in my own life and faith. I needed to experience for myself that "The Warrior's Advance" is indeed a path that leads to discovering and empowering the warrior within.

WARRIOR KING

The LORD will march forth like a mighty hero; he will come out like a warrior, full of fury. He will shout his battle cry and crush all his enemies.
ISAIAH 42:13 NLT

The boat arrived carrying a valiant warrior and his small group of faithful followers. As the warrior stepped out onto the beach, he was immediately surrounded by a fierce, demonic military force, six thousand strong. But only the brave warrior saw the evil battalion; the others didn't have eyes to see into that realm. At least not yet. Instead, they saw one naked man on his knees, a crazed look in his eyes, shackles and broken chains around his wrists and ankles. The evil was so heavy and thick you could smell its pungent odor all along the shore. Standing fearlessly, the brave warrior asked the general of the ghastly army, "What is your name?" The general replied, "Legion." Then something astonishing and unexpected happened. Rather than launching a full-out attack, the evil force—including their general—started begging the courageous warrior to not destroy them but instead to give them a way of escape. Six thousand troops surrendering to one!

Sounds like something out of a Hollywood movie, doesn't it? That story, however, is right out of Luke 8, and it is a great picture of Warrior Jesus in action. Just for the record, in Roman times, a legion was a body of well-disciplined soldiers, consisting of more than six thousand men. So here we have Warrior Jesus going out of His way to take on six thousand powerful evil angels in order to set a captive free from the clutches of the Evil One. Clearly, we can learn about the ways of a spiritual warrior by looking no further than Jesus Christ.

Have you ever really thought of Jesus as being a warrior? When I first heard that concept, I was skeptical. I'd always known Jesus as loving, kind, compassionate, a friend of sinners—but a warrior? Somehow it sounded a little sacrilegious. But, according to the apostle John, Jesus' mission on Earth was to invade enemy territory so that "He might destroy the works of the devil" (1 John 3:8). When Jesus came to this Earth, He ushered in the kingdom of heaven by waging war against the kingdom of darkness and its forces. Jesus modeled the stand, walk, and war process every day: He *stood* on the truth that He was God's beloved Son, He *walked* out His mission in the Spirit each day, and He waged *war* in the spiritual realm by calling sinners to repentance, confronting and casting out evil spirits, healing the sick, and, finally, by crushing the enemies of sin and death at the cross. Jesus was a warrior with a life-giving and eternal purpose. His enemies feared Him—and they still do!

So before we start our journey through Ephesians, let's open the book of Luke and go back to the battlefield with our Warrior King for a few moments. After Jesus was baptized with water and filled with the Holy Spirit (Luke 3:22–24), the Spirit led Him into the wilderness for His showdown with Satan. Jesus had been fasting for forty days, and Satan chose this moment, when Jesus was at His weakest point physically, to attack. (The timing of his attacks remains one of Satan's favorite strategies.) The Evil One went at Jesus with the same three types of temptation that worked so well against Adam and Eve—lust, greed, and pride. In Jesus' case, all three of Satan's attempts failed miserably. Jesus pulled out the sword of the Spirit, the Word of God, and struck down Satan with its truths. Realizing he was outmatched, Satan "departed from Him until an *opportune time*" (Luke 4:13, emphasis added). The battle-tested Warrior was now ready for His mission.

> **Battle Strategy:** Our enemy is an opportunist. He prowls around like a lion looking to devour weak prey (1 Peter 5:8), so when you are physically worn out or sick, or mentally and emotionally drained, those are opportune times for him to strike. Pray for more of God's strength in those difficult times—and be ready to strike back with His Word as the Spirit leads you. Just like Jesus did.

FEARLESS

Luke's biography of Warrior Jesus continues. Not long after He resisted Satan's temptations, Jesus was in the synagogue of Nazareth, and the people "were astonished at His teaching, for His word was with authority" (v. 32). There, in the synagogue, Jesus encountered a man possessed by a demon. Recognizing Jesus, the foul spirit cried out, "Did You come to destroy us? I know who You are—the Holy One of God!" (v. 24). Jesus spoke boldly to that demon: "Be quiet, and come out of him" (v. 35). In other words, shut up and get out! The demon obeyed, and the people were awestruck by Jesus' authority and power.

Then Jesus went to Simon Peter's house and learned that Simon's mother-in-law was sick with a burning fever. "So [Jesus] stood over her and rebuked the fever, and it left her" (v. 39). But Jesus' work for the day wasn't done. At sunset He healed a multitude, and "demons also came out of many" (v. 41). One by one Jesus took on these fallen angels, and as He defeated them, He set free the individuals they had been tormenting.

Think back now to the story of Legion. When Jesus cast out the demons, they made a curious request. They begged Jesus to not cast them into the abyss but to instead let them enter the swine grazing nearby. According to Luke, Jesus "permitted them" (8:32). The demons entered the swine, and they ran down a hill into a lake and drowned! But we have learned that angels are eternal, so the angels/demons couldn't have perished with the swine. So it appears that Jesus delivered the man, but left the legion of demons to fight another day. Why? The answer is simple: it wasn't time yet. The day is set for the battle to end. On that day Jesus will return on a white horse, leading His angel armies, wearing a robe dipped in blood, having a sharp sword come out of His mouth, and destroying all His enemies (Revelation 19:11–21). Only God knows when that day will come. In the meantime, the battle rages on.

Thankfully, in His brief time on Earth, Jesus modeled perfectly for us what the life of a Spirit-filled warrior looks like: He rose early, spent time with His Father, and then went out to fight the good fight in the power of the Holy Spirit (see Mark 1). Jesus always knew the right weapon to use to thwart or undo the Devil's work. If mercy and grace were called for, He extended those; if healing were needed, He restored; if a demon were involved, He cast it out. Jesus exercised His authority and overcame evil with good (Romans 12:21).

Jesus also battled Satan in defense of truth, and, sadly, many of those battles involved Jewish religious leaders who were operating under the adversary's influence. These scribes and Pharisees were self-righteous, prideful men who had strayed from God's path and were putting heavy burdens on the Jewish people that God never intended His followers to carry. Pawns of the Evil One and threatened by Jesus, these leaders— shockingly—wanted Him dead. Even though He was well aware of their evil intent, Jesus did not hide. Instead, He boldly and consistently confronted them about their hypocrisy as He warned His followers about them. In Matthew 23, Jesus unleashed a fierce rebuke of the scribes and Pharisees, calling them "hypocrites," "son[s] of hell," "blind guides," "fools," "whitewashed tombs," and "a brood of vipers" (see vv. 13, 15, 16, 17, 27, 33). Yikes! No wonder they wanted Him dead: He was bad for temple business! But Jesus knew that His religious opponents were under the spell of the Wicked One and that—like the ill, crippled, and possessed—they, too, needed Him to rescue them.

Jesus was a fearless spiritual Warrior, and every courageous act He did, He did because of His immense love for each of us. He loved us enough to go to war for us against every form of evil, and He ultimately gave His life on the battlefield (Calvary) to save us from the consequences of our sin. Jesus was crucified, died, was buried, rose from the dead, and then ascended to the throne at the right hand of God from which He now rules the universe: Jesus ran His race victoriously. Astonishingly, He invites us to take up the battle on Earth where He left off. When we accept His invitation, we can be confident warriors because of His promise: "I am with you always, even to the end of the age" (Matthew 28:20).

A CALL TO ARMS

You therefore, my son, be strong in the grace that is in Christ Jesus. And the things that you have heard from me among many witnesses, commit these to faithful men who will be able to teach others also. You therefore must endure hardship as a good soldier of Jesus Christ. No one engaged in warfare entangles himself with the affairs of this life, that he may please him who enlisted him as a soldier.

2 TIMOTHY 2:1–4

These verses are God's call to every warrior as well as our commissioning. And Paul was very straightforward: "You... must endure hardship as a good soldier of Jesus Christ." There is no way to misinterpret that. Paul was telling us that we are soldiers engaged in all-out spiritual warfare. Our options are to get on board with that or raise the white flag of surrender and miss out on God's mission for our lives.

I looked up the Greek definition for *soldier* as it is used in the verses above, and there it was: "to select as a warrior."[2] The word *warfare* in that passage means "to serve in a military campaign"[3] and "to lead soldiers to war or to battle: to fight."[4] These definitions describe Jesus' warrior mission. I submit to you that our mission is the same: to destroy the work of the devil just as Jesus did. Our Commander's orders are for us to proclaim the good news, pray for and lay hands on the sick, cast out demons—simply put—to help set the captives free (see Matthew 10:8, Mark 16:15–18). Jesus enlists us in His army to battle against the Enemy, and we are to fight in His strength with courage and faith as He leads the charge from heaven's throne.

I see five directives for the warrior in those verses from 2 Timothy 2: 1) Be strong in Christ's grace; 2) Teach God's truth to other faithful men; 3) Endure hardship; 4) Engage in warfare; 5) Don't get entangled in the traps of this world. Our obedience will please our Commander.

The Lord calls His warriors to trust Him and to stand strong for His kingdom no matter what we encounter, no matter what He requires of us, no matter how difficult the path becomes. We can endure hardship knowing that we have the Commander of heaven's armies leading, guiding, and empowering us. We are more than conquerors (Romans 8:37); we can do all things through Christ who strengthens us (Philippians 4:13). *All* things! We were called to a life of adventure and battle as we work to advance the kingdom of God.

I have found that fighting in this war means day-to-day, hand-to hand combat in the trenches. A dogfight. I wish I could tell you that I have slayed all my demons and conquered all my fears and foes, but that wouldn't be the truth. In many ways, I am still broken; I still struggle daily. Life is beautiful, but it is a battlefield. Yet knowing that Christ is always with me gives me great hope. Experiencing His peace as my greatest battles rage has sustained me in the fight. I'm no longer a casualty of war, and rather than being a victim, I'm a victor. I refuse to be an armchair warrior ever again. Active in the battle, I now worship my King more frequently and more wholeheartedly. More readily swallowing my pride, I don't hesitate to ask Him to rescue me and heal me. I pray more. I fight for my family more. And when the Enemy strikes, I fight back in the power of the Holy Spirit!

In this book I want to share some discoveries I've made on my journey. I've realized, for instance, that there is so much more to life than what we see. I am praying this book brings to you an awakening of who you are in Christ and of who is really behind a lot of the pain and suffering you experience in this life. No matter where other paths have led you in the past, I invite you to leave them all behind, fix your eyes on Jesus, and move forward on this path. On *His* path.

God created you for greatness in His kingdom. He placed a warrior Spirit within you that's waiting to be set free. I believe many of us are lying in the valley of dry bones that Ezekiel saw (Ezekiel 37), but the Lord is ready to revive a mighty army of warriors who will join Him in the good fight against evil.

STAND, WALK, AND WAR

In the next chapter, we'll set off on a study of Ephesians that shows us exactly how to stand, walk, and war as a soldier in Christ's army. And as I dug into this more, the Lord began to reveal to me that the stand, walk, and war process appears all through the Bible.

The parting of the Red Sea is a great example. The Egyptian army had Israel cornered along the bank of the sea with no visible means of escape… when Moses cried out some incredible words of faith: "Do not be afraid. Stand still, and see the salvation of the LORD, which He will accomplish for you today. For the Egyptians whom you see today, you shall see again no more forever. The LORD will fight for you, and you shall hold your peace" (Exodus 14:13–14). Moses was saying, "Let's have faith in God, wait for His instructions, and then watch Him fight on our behalf!" God then said to Moses, "Tell the children of Israel to move forward. But lift up your rod, and stretch out your hand over the sea and divide it" (vv. 15–16). So Israel *stood* still, the waters parted, God told them to start *walking*, and He went to *war* behind them. When the Egyptian army followed Israel onto the dry seabed, God released the walls of water He had held back for His people, and the Almighty drowned the entire Egyptian army. This truly is in one of the greatest stories of deliverance in the Bible. In this case, the Lord fought the battle Himself; all Israel had to do was listen to His instructions and obey. The story came to a grand crescendo on the opposite bank of the Red Sea when Israel broke into spontaneous worship, singing, "The LORD is a warrior. The LORD is His name" (Exodus 15:3 NIV). God is truly able to deliver us from any and every situation we face.

One other interesting point is that before God performed that miracle at the Red Sea, He told the people to be silent: "The LORD will fight for you, and you shall hold your peace" (Exodus 14:14). God gave Israel a similar command at Jericho. The battle strategy was to quietly march around the walls of Jericho for seven days. Joshua told the people: "You shall not shout or make any noise with your voice, nor shall a word proceed from your mouth, until the day I say to you, 'Shout!'" (Joshua 6:10). God knew that, if given the opportunity, Israel would start complaining or speaking words of unbelief about their situation, so He commanded silence. Faithless words are fuel for the Enemy. Keep that in mind in the heat of battle. Sometimes it's better to say nothing at all and simply let God work as He will.

> **Battle Strategy:** Ask God to help you guard your mouth, remembering that faithless words are fuel for the Enemy. We should be quick to listen, allowing God to give us our battle strategy and then obeying.

After all, we can't hear God when we are talking, and it is imperative that we hear Him. At the Red Sea and at Jericho, God provided the strategy that enabled Israel to procure a victory, but the people had to be in a position to hear His voice. Our relationship with God is meant to be an ongoing conversation—Father to son, Spirit to spirit. He speaks within us, so we must develop the ability to hear His voice in our day-to-day life. This skill is extremely helpful in warfare: we, God's soldiers, need His intel and direction if we are to walk in victory.

> **Battle Strategy:** Spend quality quiet time alone with Jesus. Ask questions and practice listening for His voice.

THE GRAND CANYON

It's hard to put into words how the book of Ephesians has transformed my life and reenergized my faith. I pray it will do the same for you. But before we begin this journey, let's review how this incredible book even came to be.

On his third missionary journey, the apostle Paul settled in Ephesus for two years, and there he experienced intense spiritual war. Acts 19 tells us that Ephesus was a mecca of demonic activity and that idol worship abounded. The city was home to the great temple of Artemis (aka Diana), the Greek goddess of love and fertility, and in addition to worshiping her, the Ephesians practiced magic arts. Clearly, Ephesus was Satan's playground, yet "God worked unusual miracles by the hands of Paul, so that even handkerchiefs or aprons were brought from his body to the sick, and the diseases left them and the evil spirits went out of them" (Acts 19:11–12).

Also in Ephesus were a priest and his seven sons who tried to cast a demon out of a man by invoking Jesus' name. The problem? These eight didn't know Jesus! The demons left the man and attacked the priest and his sons, beating them senseless until they ran away "naked and wounded" (v. 16). After witnessing these miraculous signs, many people in Ephesus believed and turned to the Lord: "Many of those who had practiced magic brought their books together and burned them in the sight of all" (v. 19). This was no small victory: the value of the books they burned was several million dollars by today's standards.

Satan had control over Ephesus, but when Paul came along with the gospel, he stirred up the heavenly realms and started a spiritual firestorm that caused riots and unrest. Spiritual warfare was Paul's way of life while he was in Ephesus and elsewhere. As a seasoned veteran, Paul was God's perfect choice to teach us about spiritual war.

So we are going to immerse ourselves in the profound truths of this letter in which the apostle Paul unveiled the mystery of God's amazing plan and purpose for His church. For me, the book of Ephesians holds answers to many questions I had wrestled with, and it addressed the war and called out the warrior in me. I have read that some call Ephesians "The Grand Canyon of Scripture," and, after visiting that breathtaking spot, I think that is a perfect description.

In 2011 my wife, Cindy, and I took our first trip out west and spent a week in Arizona. We stayed in Sedona, which is an incredibly beautiful town surrounded by red rock canyons and buttes. It turned out to be one of the best vacations of our lives. We felt like kids exploring the wild, wild west. On day three we made the two-hour drive to the Grand Canyon to spend the day there. When we arrived, we stopped at the visitor center for about a whole minute. I was too antsy and ready to get to that canyon. I grabbed Cindy's hand, and off we went. I will never forget approaching the rim and getting my first glimpse of that magnificent natural wonder. I was awestruck. The only word that came to mind was *majesty*! We just stood and stared at it for the longest time.

This exploration of Ephesians has been something like that for me: I recaptured my sense of wonder in the presence of our amazing God. This experience has made me feel like a child running up to the edge and encountering the magnitude of His grandeur as well as the breadth and depth of His love. My hope is that this journey will be a Grand Canyon experience for you. I pray your eyes will be opened wide to a whole new world that you may have never seen before. Take a step closer to the edge, warrior. If you look deep into this treasure-trove of Scripture, I believe you will be left with nothing else to say but "Majesty!"

Before each chapter of this book, I encourage you to read the corresponding chapter in Ephesians. Although many of the Scriptures I refer to are in this book, the letter itself is a masterpiece. Reading it will enrich your journey.

WAR ROOM DISCUSSION

1. What aspects of a warrior do you see in Jesus when He withstood Satan's temptations to sin... as He dealt with Legion... when He was in the synagogue at Nazareth... and when He rebuked the scribes and the Pharisees?

2. State your understanding of Warrior Jesus' mission on this earth and why you agree/disagree with His decision to hand the battle over to us.

3. Which of the five directives for the warrior found in 2 Timothy 2:1–4 are you least comfortable with? Why—and what will you do to grow stronger in that area?

4. What does the account of Moses leading God's people across the Red Sea on dry ground show you about the effectiveness of the progression from stand, to walk, and to war... and about the value of silence?

5. What aspect of God's creation has filled you with wonder and left you awestruck—and when, if ever, has a passage of Scripture had the same effect on you? Expect that to happen as we explore Ephesians together.

READ EPHESIANS 1

3

DELIVERED
RESCUED, REDEEMED, RESTORED

*He has delivered us from the power of darkness and
conveyed us into the kingdom of the Son of His love.*
COLOSSIANS 1:13

*In Him we have redemption through His blood, the
forgiveness of sins, according to the riches of His grace.*
EPHESIANS 1:7

I awoke suddenly to the morning's piercing sunlight coming through
the windshield and blinding my bloodshot eyes. Totally disoriented,
my head pounding, I slowly realized the sound I kept hearing was
traffic whizzing by.

Where am I? What on earth happened last night? As the alcohol-
induced fog began to clear slightly, I realized I was lying across the seat
of my pickup truck. I raised my aching head enough to see I was on the
side of a busy road in Columbus, Ohio.

God, what have I done? Slowly, I recalled the screeching sound of
metal on metal as I had slammed into the guardrail in the wee hours of
the morning. The impact had thrown me headlong into the passenger
side door, and it was lights out. I had done it again—gotten totally
inebriated and passed out behind the wheel. I staggered out of my
totaled truck and looked over the guardrail to discover I was but a few
feet away from plunging into the Olentangy River far below.

Oh, I knew the power of darkness well. My life was shrouded in it: alcohol abuse, drugs, promiscuous sex. I was a dead man walking before I gave my life to Christ in 1997. Before then, if I had died or killed myself (which I thought about on occasion), I would have been forever separated from the God I now love and cherish. Thinking about it makes me want to cry. Long before I gave my life to Christ—and even though I was utterly undeserving—God rescued me countless times. And that is exactly what deliverance means: rescue.

I probably should have died that dreary night in Columbus, but the Lord wasn't finished with me yet. If you are reading these words, know that He isn't finished with you either. If you haven't accepted Christ as your Savior, I pray you will—soon. You are needed in the battle, my friend. If you have named Jesus your Lord, then we are both beneficiaries of the greatest rescue ever. Far surpassing the parting of the Red Sea or the walls falling at Jericho, the cross of Christ reigns supreme as the ultimate rescue for all mankind and for all time! Christ's death for our sins and His resurrection mean we get a new start, a new heart, and a solid Rock on which to build our lives as we walk the warrior path.

So it's time to start on the path through Ephesians, and we'll begin with the verse that opened this chapter. Ephesians 1:7 speaks of the great deliverance that God procured for us through the sacrifice of His Son. Jesus bought our redemption by paying the debt for our sinfulness that we could never pay; then Jesus blazed the path to heaven that only He could blaze. Jesus' death on the cross and His resurrection three days later mean that we can stand completely forgiven of all our sins, past, present, and future by accepting Him as our Savior.

Jesus chose the warrior path despite knowing it would require from Him the ultimate sacrifice—His very life. Aware from the beginning of time that His mission was to set the captives free, at the appointed hour Jesus allowed Himself to be led like a lamb to the slaughter (Isaiah 53:7). Then He laid down His life, rescuing us from sin and death, from eternal separation from God. The life of the spiritual warrior begins where Christ's earthly life ended: at the cross.

Although Calvary was the greatest rescue ever, God's deliverance doesn't end there; it only begins there. For many of my years as a Christian, though, I kept looking for that one great deliverance that would make me feel complete and that would make the majority of my problems disappear. I didn't understand that deliverance is the lifelong process of learning to trust God completely. That kind of trust can only be developed over time—rescue by rescue.

The more often we allow God to deliver us from our trials and fears, the deeper our roots of trust in Him grow. As we spend time at His feet, immersed in His words of life, we gradually come to the realization that we are not who we once were. We have discovered a warrior inside of us. Jesus, our Deliverer and the Lion of Judah, now resides in our hearts.

Jesus taught us to pray for such deliverance by giving us the model prayer that ends with "Deliver us from the Evil One" (Luke 11:1–4). That request tells us two truths: first, the Lord wants us to take seriously the battle with the Evil One and, second, we will need Almighty God to deliver us many times over! We should never attempt to fight against the Enemy in our own strength. Remember that God is a warrior, that His Spirit lives within us, and that He will fight our battles with us and for us. Whenever the war rages, He will always come through for His faithful ones. Satan and his army are powerful, but they are no match for our warrior God.

SAINT

To the saints who are in Ephesus...
EPHESIANS 1:1

Saints? In Ephesus? Remember, these are the same folks not far removed from a life of idol worship, the practice of magic arts, and bondage to the prince of darkness. Paul called them saints. Already?

When I first started writing this section, I actually skipped Ephesians 1:1–2 and went right to verse 3. Then during church one

Sunday, as we entered into worship, the Lord clearly told me that I had missed *saint*. Earlier that morning in Bible study, Darrell had said, "God has a big eraser" (referring to how He deals with our past sin) and quoted this verse: "As far as the east is from the west, so far has He removed our transgressions from us" (Psalm 103:12). Darrell said that no matter what we've done in the past, God has—in Christ—erased our sin and removed it as if it never happened: "I have blotted out, like a thick cloud, your transgressions, and like a cloud, your sins" (Isaiah 44:22).

As I stood there contemplating all of this, the worship team started playing an amazing rendition of "It Is Well with My Soul." As they proceeded, our church began to erupt in an outpouring of triumph as we sang these truths:

> My sin—oh, the bliss of this glorious thought!—
> My sin, not in part but the whole,
> Is nailed to the cross, and I bear it no more,
> Praise the Lord, praise the Lord, O my soul!

In that moment, I realized that we are saints the instant we receive Christ. There is no waiting period. There is no work to be done. Jesus already did it. We were once lost in our sins, but Christ paid for all our sins on the cross. Every sin we ever committed and every sin we will ever commit was nailed to that wood and paid for. Believing anything else is an insult to our Lord Jesus and diminishes what He has accomplished for us.

Now, the Greek word Paul used for *saint* is *hagios* which is actually the same word translated *holy* in verse 4. Our past life is behind us; we are now holy saints set apart to battle against evil and to carry the gospel truth into a desperate, hopeless world. The church in Ephesus wasn't some special, elite group; they were former enemies of God just like you and me. Accepting Christ as their Savior qualified them as saints. The same is true for us.

Being a saint, however, doesn't mean we won't ever sin again. It means the blood of Christ has washed away all our sin. So now, when we sin, we can go boldly before God's throne, confess and repent of our sins, and receive His complete forgiveness.

I know it may sound strange—and it did to me at first—but we are now holy warriors, set apart for kingdom work as we serve in the army of the King!

IN CHRIST

... and faithful in Christ Jesus.
EPHESIANS 1:1

Growing up, I loved football, and I still do. When I was about seven years old, my dad took me to a Cincinnati Bengals game, and I was completely awestruck when I stepped into that stadium. I felt like I had entered the gladiator's arena—and I was hooked for life. Afterward, I played imaginary football games in my backyard where I would not only throw, but also catch the game-winning touchdown pass as the invisible crowd roared! I dreamed of being one of those gladiators.

And, soon, I was! At eight years old, I entered that gladiator arena when I joined my first Pop Warner team. I learned pretty quickly, though, that the real thing was far more difficult than my backyard Super Bowl victories. Before I could become the gridiron legend I had imagined, I needed some actual training. I needed to submit to the coach and learn his whole playbook; I needed physical conditioning for stamina; I needed to learn basic blocking and tackling as well as how to work as part of a team. I remember doing calisthenics, running laps, and doing practice drills on hot August days, in full pads, weeks before we even had our first scrimmage. The training was grueling—but it was absolutely necessary. When the real games finally began, I was prepared and confident when I took the field.

We need this same kind of basic knowledge and training—and the resulting sense of being ready and confident—for the spiritual war we can't avoid. If you are like me, you probably want to just put on the armor of God and charge into the battle—but that would be a mistake. You see, as we've already discussed, our opponent is strategic, his team is well-trained, and they play dirty. Furthermore, they believe they have a winning game plan and our defeat is sure.

To be victorious, then, we must first believe in the unconquerable greatness of our omnipotent God. Beyond that, we need to learn our position: we need to know what is called *positional truth*, the truth about our position in Christ's kingdom. In the first three chapters of Ephesians, Paul laid a strong foundation of this truth that we must confidently *stand* on. We can't make strategic battle decisions—or life decisions—based solely on our feelings or our random and fickle thoughts. Doing so will lead to defeat. Instead, we must stand firm on the positional truths of who the Bible says we become at the moment of our conversion. We need to study, meditate on, and develop a deep understanding and firm belief in this positional truth before we move on. Only then will we stand strong in the battles ahead.

So who are we at the moment of our conversion? In Ephesians 1:1 Paul said that we are *in Christ*. In fact, the apostle said "in Christ," "in Him," or "in the Beloved" eleven times in Ephesians 1 alone. I think he was trying to tell us that *in Christ* is an amazing place to be, and appropriating all that it means to be in Christ will indeed transform and revolutionize our lives as we go forward on the warrior path.

Being in Christ is our new identity, and Paul put it this way: "if anyone is *in Christ*, he is a new creation; old things have passed away; behold, all things have become new" (2 Corinthians 5:17, emphasis added). Believing that statement is crucial for our progress on the warrior path. In fact, the degree to which we appropriate our new identity in Christ will greatly determine the impact we will have for God's kingdom. Our position, our potential, our purpose, and our power all hinge on how firmly we stand on the promises of who we are in Him. We can't miss this. We are not the same person we once were, yet the Enemy will work overtime to get us to default to our old lives and our old way of thinking. If, however, we consistently renew our minds by regularly reviewing the truth of who we are in Christ, we will overcome the Evil One.

Let's now look at the meaning of the word *in: denoting (fixed) position (in place, time or state); give self wholly to.*[1] "In Christ" is our fixed position, and the more firmly we stand on that truth, the more effective we will be in battle. Our Warrior King battled against evil and conquered sin and death so that we can be reconciled to God, our eternal future secure in Him. Our job is to believe, receive, and immerse ourselves in the truth of what our heavenly Father has done for us. We can only become the warriors He created us to be if we understand that—by His grace evident on the Cross—we have made the first-string on His winning team. We are in Christ!

"EVERY SPIRITUAL BLESSING"

Blessed be the God and Father of our Lord Jesus Christ, who has blessed us with *every spiritual blessing* in the heavenly places in Christ, just as He *chose* us in Him before the foundation of the world, that we should be *holy* and *without blame* before Him in love, having predestined us to *adoption* as sons by Jesus Christ to Himself ... by which He made us *accepted* in the Beloved... In Him we have redemption through His blood, the *forgiveness* of sins, according to the riches of His grace... being *predestined* ... *sealed* with the Holy Spirit of promise.

EPHESIANS 1:3-7, 11, 13 (emphasis added)

In the verses above, Paul identified eight heavenly blessings that come with being in Christ. Discovering these truths—fifteen years into my Christian walk—grounded me in my faith. And Paul's is only a partial list of the incredible blessings we inherit in Christ, yet what a list it is!

According to Paul, in Christ, we are chosen, holy, blameless, adopted, accepted, forgiven, predestined, and sealed by the Holy Spirit. So let's unpack each of these gifts of grace, these blessings we could never earn:

- **Chosen:** Just as our Lord Jesus consulted with the Father and then put together His ragtag team of disciples, so He handpicked us to be soldiers in His army. It's not like grade school when the best were chosen right away while others only made the team by default. No, God chose us to be part of His elite forces even before time began.

- **Holy:** This word means "sacred: physically pure: separated from sin and therefore consecrated to God."[1] We can't earn holiness, but we can't go before God until we are holy. Our holy God cannot tolerate the presence of sin, so He made us holy through Jesus' blood. God's will was for us to be made holy—to be "separated from sin"—by the forgiveness made available by Jesus' sacrifice of Himself on the cross, a blood sacrifice of the perfect Lamb, once for all time (see Hebrews 10:10).

- **Blameless:** Because of the matchless work of Christ, God now sees us as faultless, and the Enemy's accusations have no foundation. In Christ we are declared "not guilty" on any and all charges. If your past is really dark, meditate on verses about being holy and blameless so that you can dismiss the Enemy's lies. Our past sin was atoned for and blotted out. So Satan has no legal grounds to bring it up again. Don't let him!

- **Adopted:** Many people have endured great pain and even abuse from their parents, and none of us escapes our youth without any wounds. Parents' words hurt and can even cripple us, their neglect can undermine and weaken us, and inexcusable physical abuse leaves psychological scars that don't heal even after the physical wounds do. Whatever you experienced growing up in your home, God can bring healing. In fact, God Himself *is* the cure: as heavenly Father, He claims us as His sons and daughters. He can re-parent us and bring to us a wholeness greater than we can imagine. Consider that Jesus was so close to the Father that He called Him *Abba*, which is a term expressing a warm father-son relationship (see Mark 14:36 and Galatians 4:6), and we are free to call God *Abba* as well! God is our true Father: He loves us unconditionally and wants the highest good for our lives. We are kingdom sons, heirs of God, and co-heirs with Christ: "You did not receive the spirit of bondage again to fear, but you received the Spirit of adoption [sonship] by whom we cry out, 'Abba, Father'" (Romans 8:15).

- **Accepted:** We are blessed with special honor and highly favored by our King. Someone has said, "We are graced with grace," and I love the sound of that. I love the *truth* of that! Our loving God accepts us—with all of our fears, failures, sins, and shortcomings—because we are in Christ, and we are in Christ because of Jesus' death on our behalf. We can quit trying to be good enough and simply go to God just as we are—and He will always welcome us as His beloved.

- **Forgiven:** Christ has broken every chain of sin that held us down and set us free by shedding His own blood as the perfect sin sacrifice! We are pardoned, delivered, and released from bondage to sin. Also, with our own debit sheet wiped clean, we are now free to forgive others, to extend to them the same mercy we have received from God.

- **Predestined:** God created each of us and designed a plan for our life that is uniquely ours. He set us apart for "good works, which God prepared beforehand that we should [do] them" (Ephesians 2:10). David wrote, "Your eyes saw my substance, being yet unformed. And in Your book they all were written, the days fashioned for me, when as yet there were none of them"

(Psalm 139:16). Before time began, God dreamed us up and mapped out our lives. Nothing that happens in our lives takes Him by surprise. Besides, Jesus is the Author of life, and we can trust that He has written a good story for us. We must seek Him with all of our heart to discover our God-written mission.

- **Sealed:** Not only are we kingdom sons, hidden in Christ, but God has also set His seal upon us by giving us the fullness of His Holy Spirit. The word *seal* refers to the way a king would mark documents or laws as authentically His. Taking his signet ring that was engraved with his name or an identifying mark, the king would put soft clay on the document and then use his ring to make an impression in it. When the clay dried, the document was sealed, its words were law, and those laws couldn't be changed. So when God sealed us, He put His stamp on us for all eternity. This seal—the presence of the Spirit in us—is our guarantee that we are God's property and beneficiaries of all His promises.

This partial list of blessings we have in Christ is quite astounding, isn't it? These are part of our inheritance as Christ followers, and we can stand in complete confidence that we will receive and experience them.

Keep in mind, however, that your Enemy is determined to keep you from fully appropriating the kingdom life God has for you. The Evil One and his minions will lie, confuse, and create diversions to keep you from discovering the whole truth about who you are in Christ. It may take you some time to bring down the mountain of lies Satan has put in your way, but stay the course. As you pursue God with all your heart, He will make sure you receive your full inheritance.

God always wins, so we win with God: "He who is in you is greater than he that is in the world" (1 John 4:4). Satan relentlessly attacks the Lord's people in hopes that we will grow weary and never completely understand that, in Christ, we really are world changers. That truth reminds me of one of my favorite statements by John Eldredge:

The story of your life is the long and brutal assault on your heart by the one who knows what you could be and fears it.[2]

The Enemy has relentlessly assaulted your heart because he fears your becoming the warrior God created you to be. Never retreat! Don't let him win. After all, as Paul put it in Romans 8:37, you are more than a conqueror!

> **Battle Strategy:** When the Enemy whispers that you don't measure up, tell him emphatically, "No, Satan! I most certainly do! Let me tell you who I am! I am chosen, holy, blameless, adopted, accepted, redeemed, forgiven, predestined, and sealed by the Holy Spirit in Christ—and in Jesus' name, I command you to flee!"

WOUNDED WARRIOR

He reached down from heaven and rescued me...
He rescued me from my powerful enemies, from those
who hated me and were too strong for me.
PSALM 18:16–17 NLT

... the gospel of your salvation.
EPHESIANS 1:13

I took a surprise right hook to the face and hit the ground hard.

News of the fight apparently spread quickly because the excited crowd surrounded us in just a matter of seconds. Now the main event could begin.

"Get up and fight, you coward!" he taunted. The funny thing is, that guy who was standing over me had told me, minutes earlier at the party, that I should break up with his sister because she was seeing other guys.

So I did. It was, I realized at that point, a setup. And the toughest kid in eighth grade was ready to tear me to shreds. I sat there paralyzed by fear.

"Get up, you coward," he repeated. And I sat there in my shame. After repeating himself several more times, he finally gave up, rattled off a few disparaging remarks, and walked away. The crowd, laughing and sneering, followed him. I got up, brushed away tears, and walked home alone. The voice of the Enemy was ringing in my ears not only that night, but for years to come: "*You* are a coward."

That incident was a direct assault of the Enemy, intended to wound and emasculate a young, insecure teen. The arrow hit its target with deadly pinpoint accuracy. Prowling around like a roaring lion that night, Satan pounced on weak prey and delivered a deep heart wound. That painful mantra didn't simply fade away; instead, I owned it.

I'm sure you have stories like that yourself, and yours may be much worse than the one I just shared. Whatever wounds we have experienced in battle, we must bring them to Jesus and allow Him to heal us and restore us. This is what David meant when he said about God, "He restores my soul" (Psalm 23:2). To be wholehearted in our faith and to effectively fight for the freedom of others, we must invite Jesus to restore our wounds.

After all—as you've probably heard it said—you can't give away what you don't possess. As I began to grow in my Christian faith, I wanted to help others, but I was still so wounded and battle-scarred that I wasn't in any shape to do so. The Enemy kept me so bound up by past mistakes that I had little energy left to reach out. I needed healing, restoration, and rescue myself. Even though I have come a long way, I still desperately need God's grace daily.

I'm like Bill Murray in one of my favorite comedies, *What About Bob?* where he says to his therapist, "Gimmee, gimmee, gimmee! I need, I need, I need!" It's funny, but it's also very true. We are needy people, and on this side of heaven, we always will be to some degree. But God knows our wounds and exactly how and when He will bring healing. As we pursue His heart, He can heal ours.

Key to our healing and recovery from heart wounds is understanding the meaning of salvation in the New Testament. There, the Greek word for *salvation* is *soteria*, and its verb form is *sozo*. *Sozo* is translated "to save" and, many times, "to heal." So both *salvation* and *healing* mean health, deliverance, rescue, and to make whole. I used to think *salvation* meant that I had given my life to Christ so I was saved from eternal damnation. End of story. As amazing as the initial experience of salvation is, that moment is actually only the beginning. God's intention is to restore the whole man into the creature He originally designed. Jesus is exactly what God had in mind when He created human beings, so His plan for all of us is Christlikeness.

Salvation, therefore, is intended to be God's deliverance or rescue of the entire man. Consider that we are threefold creatures—body, soul, and spirit—and salvation is a threefold process—being saved, delivered, and healed. At the cross, Jesus paved the way for us to receive healing by faith: our spirit was saved, our soul was delivered, and our physical body was healed. Although physical healing doesn't always occur in this life, we should have faith for healing, and we can be sure our afflictions always have a greater purpose just as the thorn in Paul's side did (see 2 Corinthians 12:7–9). Jesus intends for His warriors to be healed, whole, and holy. Just as God chose Moses to deliver Israel from four hundred years of bondage in Egypt, God sent Jesus into the world to deliver us from all we have suffered at the hand of the Enemy.

One day when I was talking to Cindy about the threefold process of salvation—being saved, delivered, and healed—she pointed out that Satan's plan is threefold as well: "The thief does not come except to steal, and to kill, and to destroy" (John 10:10). I don't think it's a coincidence that Satan's plan is the antithesis of salvation: spirit = steal, soul = kill, body = destroy. It's so predictable: Satan always offers a counterfeit to everything God wants to do in our lives.

In my case, my past sin, my lack of knowledge of God's Word, and the schemes of the Enemy made the path to overcoming my wounds a difficult journey: "My people are destroyed for lack of knowledge" (Hosea 4:6). The battle was brutal on my heart when I was a young man. Battling low self-worth, unsaved, and unprepared for what the world, my flesh, and the Devil would throw at me, I opened up my life to a lot of spiritual and emotional bondage through drugs, alcohol, and promiscuous sex. The result was years of guilt and shame, which was exactly the Enemy's plan. Thankfully, God had a better plan. He was not going to let me stay in that condition. From the beginning, His plan for me—and for you—was restoration.

RESTORATION

The truth is—we are all broken. Our hearts have been shattered by past mistakes, various forms of abuse, lost loved ones, and the list goes on. But an even greater truth is that Jesus is the answer to all of our brokenness. In Luke 4:18, Jesus proclaimed in His mission statement: "He has sent me to heal the brokenhearted, To proclaim liberty to the captives." The Lord knows and understands our brokenness. He also knows exactly what is needed to make us whole again. After all, Jesus came to "destroy the works of the devil" (1 John 3:8) and set the captives free!

Though we are brand-new creations at the moment of our salvation, our restoration is a process that unfolds as we walk with Him day by day: "He who has begun a good work in you will complete it until the day of Jesus Christ" (Philippians 1:6). We must invite Him into our brokenness so He can do what only He can do—restore our souls. God says in His Word: "I have loved you with an everlasting love; I have drawn you with unfailing kindness. I will build you up again, and you... will be rebuilt" (Jeremiah 31:3-4). God is in the restoration business, and Jesus has already paid the cost for the work that needs to be done. As we spend time at the Master's feet, immersed in His presence, He will restore us to health and heal us of our wounds (Jeremiah 30:17).

Consider what Jesus did for three people we meet in Luke 8 and what their role was in the restoration process. First, Luke said the demoniac (whom we met in chapter 2) "fell down before Jesus" (v. 28). Next, a desperate father approached Jesus about his dying daughter and "fell down at Jesus' feet and begged him" (v. 41). Finally, a woman with a twelve-year flow of blood "came from behind and touched the border of His garment" (v. 44). Desperately, all three humbled themselves before Jesus. Then, after his restorative encounter with the Lord, the demoniac was "sitting at the feet of Jesus, clothed and in his right mind" and "healed" (*sozo* in vv. 35–36). Jesus had instructed the distressed father to "only believe, and she will be made well," and his daughter was (vv. 50). Finally, Jesus had told the bleeding woman, "Your faith has made you well" (v. 48).

In all three cases, healing seems to be connected to kneeling. So maybe we need to ask ourselves some questions: How desperate are we to be restored or to see others restored? How much time have we spent humbly at the Master's feet? Do we have faith that God can heal us and deliver us from anything? It seems the three-step restoration process of being saved, delivered, and healed sometimes requires on our part the trio of desperation, humility, and faith.

The only hope that these three seekers had was—Christ! Satan had *stolen* control of the demoniac's spirit; he had *killed* the young girl; and he had *destroyed* the health of the woman with the flow of blood. In all three cases, however, Jesus completely stopped and reversed Satan's steal, kill, and destroy missions.

> **Battle Strategy:** Show God that you are desperate to be restored—body, soul, and spirit. Spend time humbly at His feet and be steadfast in your faith, believing Jesus can and will restore you in His timing. Pray healing and restoration verses over your life and the lives of those you love.

THE INHERITANCE

In Him also we have obtained an inheritance.
EPHESIANS 1:11

You were sealed with the Holy Spirit of promise,
who is the guarantee of our inheritance.
EPHESIANS 1:13-14

What are the riches of the glory of His inheritance in the saints...
EPHESIANS 1:18

In Ephesians 1 alone, Paul spoke of the glorious "inheritance" of God three times. He didn't want us to miss out on the incredible riches we have in Christ. Paul knew we could easily overlook that inheritance, forsake it, or settle for the scraps our Enemy—the Deceiver—would give us. We do have choices: will we be a slave of Satan or captive to Christ, a prisoner of this world or co-heir with the King?

A friend of mine told me a parable about a rich man who died and left priceless treasures behind. The time arrived to auction them all off, and the whole town was present and buzzing with excitement. The auctioneer stepped up to the podium and announced the first item that was up for bid. Sitting front and center, on an easel, was a portrait that the rich man had painted of his only son. Everyone could see it was a very amateur painting, so the auctioneer opened the bidding at $10. The gardener of the rich man's estate, who had known and loved the son, immediately raised his hand to bid. The auctioneer asked, "Do I hear $20?" No bids. After a moment, the auctioneer asked, "Are there no other bids for the portrait of this man's only son?" Nothing. "Going once, going twice—SOLD! To the gardener for $10," and the auctioneer slammed down his gavel.

Then the auctioneer said, "That concludes the auction. Thank you all for coming today." Stunned, everyone looked around in disbelief when someone in the crowd yelled out, "What about all these other treasures?" The auctioneer replied, "It was the rich man's desire that whoever bought the portrait of his only son, would get his entire inheritance as well."

That is the offer God extends to us: accept His Son and receive the whole inheritance, the entire kingdom! Every benefit. Every spiritual blessing. Everything.

Don't settle for less.

WISDOM AND REVELATION

[I pray] that the God of our Lord Jesus Christ, the Father of glory, may give you the spirit of wisdom and revelation in the knowledge of Him, the eyes of your understanding being enlightened; that you may know what is the hope of His calling, what are the riches of His glorious inheritance in the saints.

EPHESIANS 1:15-18

I can imagine Paul, working by candlelight in his prison cell, writing his letter on parchment as the Holy Spirit pours the words into his heart. Perhaps Paul paused after finishing the first section, then started scrawling a Spirit-led prayer (Ephesians 1:15-23) asking God to open the hearts and minds of His people, so they would fully grasp the kingdom life He has given them.

Paul's first prayer in Ephesians is one we should pray often for others as well as for ourselves. It's an important tactical prayer asking God for wisdom and the spiritual insight to see into the heavenly realms and to truly know Christ and the power He has made available to us for our mission. We are fighting a spiritual war, so we need spiritual vision, guidance, and power to fight effectively.

So, on our behalf, Paul petitioned God to give us "the spirit of wisdom and revelation" and to "open the eyes of [our] understanding" (vv. 17-18). Paul knew firsthand that we not only need God's wisdom

(His Word), but we also need His revelation (to hear His voice) if we are to successfully carry out our mission. Our assignment takes us behind Enemy lines, into hostile territory, so we need open communication lines at all times. Jesus promises to reveal the intel we need in order to be effective however the battle unfolds.

How does that work? Well, many times throughout our day we can find ourselves in the trenches, facing a situation that we are not sure how to handle. When we need to know in that moment what our next move should be—when we need the Lord's revelation—we pray, "Lord, how should I handle this situation at work?"; "I don't know what to do in my marriage. Please show me"; "Do You want me to confront this person directly?"; "Is this a physical sickness or a spiritual attack from the Enemy?" Whatever the circumstances, we can simply go to Jesus, ask Him specific questions, and listen for the still small voice within. This kind of communication with our Commander is crucial for effective spiritual warfare.

POWER SOURCE

The next words in Paul's prayer might be the Bible's most potent description of the magnitude of God's resurrection power. In fact, in the New Testament, there are four Greek words used for *power*, and these two verses happen to contain all four. I don't believe that occurs anywhere else in the Bible:

> That you may know... what is the exceeding greatness of His power [*dunamis*] toward us who believe, according to the working of His mighty [*ischus*] power [*kratos*] which He worked in Christ when He raised Him from the dead and seated Him at His right hand in the heavenly places, far above all principality and power [*exousia*] and might and dominion, and every name that is named. (Ephesians 1:19–21)

It's hard to fathom the omnipotence Paul tried to describe in these verses. The explosion of an atomic bomb would seem insignificant compared to the spiritual firepower talked about here. Paul was praying for us to "know" this resurrection power that was poured first into Christ and now into those of us who are in Christ. We can look around and see the greatness of God's power in creation, but nothing displays His absolute power more gloriously than when He brought His only Son back from the dead as Victor over sin and death, to rule and reign forever. God wants us to know that power experientially.

Although the passage includes four Greek words for power, we'll only focus on two of them. First, the Greek word *dunamis*—the root of our English word *dynamite*—communicates God's miracle-working power, strength, and ability. Jesus used this same *power* word in Acts when He spoke this amazing prophecy:

> "You shall receive power when the Holy Spirit has come upon you; and you shall be witnesses to Me in Jerusalem, and in all Judea and Samaria, and to the end of the earth." (Acts 1:8)

Jesus let His followers know that power was coming!

Second, the *power* word *exousia* denotes great authority. The principalities and powers (*exousia*) mentioned in verse 20 refer to Satan's army. It is our right to act and use *dunamis* because Jesus has delegated to us the authority to do so:

> "Behold, I give you the authority [*exousia*] to trample on serpents and scorpions, and over all the power of the enemy, and nothing shall by any means hurt you." (Luke 10:19)

Clearly, Jesus handed over the power of attorney and equipped His disciples for battle. He began by delegating power first to His twelve disciples (Luke 9:1); next, to seventy others (Luke 10:1); and then, on the Day of Pentecost, to every believer (Acts 2:1–4). Hear me on this:

Jesus freely gave His early disciples His authority and power, He has done so since then, and He continues to do so today. In other words, we have available to us the same resurrection power that raised Jesus from the dead. The power of the Holy Spirit was poured out on the day of Pentecost, and it has been available to every believer ever since.

> God has put all things under the authority of Christ and has made him head over all things ... The church is his body; it is made full and complete by Christ, who fills all things everywhere with himself. (Ephesians 1:22–23 NLT)

Everything, in every realm, is now under Christ's authority. He is the Head of the church; we are His hands and feet, His body. According to God's design, the Head and the body are to work together in unity to accomplish the mission.

Thankfully, an amazing inheritance is ours, and indescribable power is available to us because the spiritual war is going to get even more interesting.

> **Note:** Read aloud the warrior declarations at the end of each chapter. Begin each line with "As a warrior in Christ, I declare that ..." and then proclaim the truth. It would be helpful to declare these truths daily for a couple of weeks until you feel you are completely grounded in them.

THE TAKEAWAY

As a warrior in Christ, I declare that …

- I am a holy saint (Ephesians 1:1).
- I am blessed with every spiritual blessing in the heavenly realms (1:3).
- I am chosen to be one of His elite warriors (1:4).
- I am blameless! The Enemy has no grounds to accuse me (1:4).
- I am a beloved son, adopted into God's family (1:5).
- I am accepted in Him just as I am; I am graced with grace (1:6).
- I am redeemed. Jesus ransomed me, delivered me from sin, and set me free from its eternal consequences by His blood (1:7–8).
- God has a divine purpose and plan for my life (1:11).
- I am saved (*sozo*) for eternity, yet God is healing and restoring me daily (1:13).
- God has sealed me with the Holy Spirit, His stamp of approval (1:13).
- I am God's possession, purchased with the blood of His Son (1:14).
- I have direct access to Jesus for spiritual wisdom and insight (1:17).
- I have confident hope in His calling on my life (1:18).
- I have a rich and glorious inheritance along with all the saints (1:18).
- I have God's incredible resurrection power and authority within me (1:19–20).

Father, I take my stand on all of Your promises today. Thank You for rescuing me, redeeming me, and placing me in Christ. Through Him I receive every spiritual blessing that You bestow. I also thank You that I am saved, redeemed, chosen, holy, blameless, an adopted son, accepted, forgiven, predestined for Your mission, and sealed by the Holy Spirit.

I pray for Your wisdom and revelation and ask that You would open my spiritual eyes and enable me to live in the hope of Your calling. I fully receive the glorious inheritance I have in You as an adopted son. Fill me, this day, with Your incredible resurrection power that You graciously make available to me by Your Spirit. In Jesus' powerful name I pray.

WAR ROOM DISCUSSION

1. What responsibilities do you feel come with the title *saint*?

2. What does it mean to you that you are in Christ? Be specific.

3. According to Paul, in Christ, we are chosen, holy, blameless, adopted, accepted, forgiven, predestined, and sealed by the Holy Spirit (Ephesians 1:3–13). Which of these interrelated blessings—all freely given to you by God Himself—do you find most meaningful at this point of your life? Why?

4. What does it mean to you personally that salvation and healing are related matters?

5. We believers have access to the resurrection power. To what ends does God want us to exercise that power while we are on this earth? Name at least three specific ways you can use God's power for His kingdom work.

READ EPHESIANS 2

4

VICTORIOUS
SEATED WITH CHRIST

Thanks be to God, who gives us the victory
through our Lord Jesus Christ.
1 CORINTHIANS 15:57

You He made alive, who were dead in trespasses and sins.
EPHESIANS 2:1

"O praise the One who paid my debt and raised this life up from the dead." That line is from the old hymn "Jesus Paid It All" —and what a sweet proclamation of our God-given victory in life it is! One morning I included this hymn in the worship set, and as we repeated that refrain over and over for several minutes, a sense of triumphant and victorious power swept through our church. Afterward, a friend of mine said, "Those words stopped me in my tracks—and set me free."

Those words should stop us in our tracks. We are all in debt to our holy God because of our sin, and we who are spiritually penniless and morally bankrupt could never pay that debt. Either sinless Jesus paid up on our behalf, or we were all going down. Jesus paid. Dearly. Willingly. And according to the eternal plan. As the prophet Isaiah foretold, "the LORD has laid on Him the iniquity of us all" (Isaiah 53:6). When I think of the enormity of the sin I myself have committed—and I am just one of the billions of sinners who have walked the planet—what Jesus did is beyond my comprehension. He footed the entire bill. He paid my sin debt and yours with His blood. And our debts are paid in full.

When Ephesians 2:1 says, "You He made alive," Paul meant that, at the moment of our conversion, we are spiritually resurrected and fully ready to start our walk in the Spirit. Debt-free and full of new life in Christ, we start to breathe freely, but we do have to clean up the carnage from the war even as we continue to fight the Enemy. He will compel us to either battle to maintain our newfound freedom—or retreat. The Enemy believes he can make us wave the white flag of surrender. As William Wallace asked his men in *Braveheart*, "What will you do with your freedom? Will you fight?" Will you? Will I? The fight will be intense because—I hate to be the bearer of bad news—the Devil isn't the only threat. Other enemies lurk in the shadows to try to take out the spiritual warrior.

WORLD WAR III

You once walked according to the course of this world, according to the prince of the power of the air, the spirit who now works in the sons of disobedience, among whom also we all once conducted ourselves in the lusts of our flesh, fulfilling the desires of the flesh and of the mind, and were by nature children of wrath, just as the others.

EPHESIANS 2:2–3

As the verses above indicate, three enemies are after a warrior's soul: the world, the flesh, and the Devil ("the prince of the power of the air"). Though Paul was describing life before salvation, these three enemies actively oppose our efforts as we, now believers, seek to move closer to God and to honor Him with our lives. So we must deal with these evil three on a daily basis, or they will too easily thwart our growth as warriors for Christ.

Satan uses both the flesh and the world to expose our weaknesses and lead us into temptation. For our protection against these Enemy attacks, God has given us full armor, which we will talk about in chapter 8. Right now let's look at our other two formidable foes.

THE WORLD

Like the Great Oz from the classic *The Wizard of Oz*, Satan is the mastermind pulling the levers behind the world's curtain. And *the world* refers to "the whole circle of earthly goods, endowments, riches, advantages, pleasures, etc., which although hollow and frail and fleeting, stir desire, seduce from God and are obstacles to the cause of Christ."[1] Self-determination, selfish ambition, materialism, and many other gods of this world seduce us and, once we succumb, produce in us an unquenchable thirst for more, dragging us away from what truly satisfies—a life with God in Christ. The world system also tries to hinder our faith-walk by keeping us discontent and therefore constantly chasing created things rather than the Creator of those things.

So instead of supporting our pursuit of a deeper relationship with our God, the world screams that we men should work long hours, climb corporate ladders, have all the latest toys and gadgets, become adventure addicts, and pursue the American Dream (whatever that is). So we work, climb, pursue, and purchase our way to a false sense of power, significance, and security. We buy into—and build our lives on—the lie that we can attain strength and confidence by means of our worldly pursuits. But that strategy never works for long. We eventually end up empty, confused, and exhausted as our materialistic kingdoms crumble around us.

Jesus asked a provocative question about this human quest for what the world values: "What profit is it to a man if he gains the whole world, and loses his own soul?" (Matthew 16:26). Jesus' brother James wrote about humility as a wise response to worldliness:

> "God opposes the proud but gives grace to the humble." So humble yourselves before God. Resist the devil, and he will flee from you. Come close to God, and God will come close to

you. Wash your hands, you sinners; purify your hearts, for your loyalty is divided between God and the world. (James 4:6–8 NLT)

Peter quoted the same Old Testament verse (Proverbs 3:34) as he also connected humility to overcoming Satan:

> Yes, all of you be submissive to one another, and be clothed with humility, for "God resists the proud, but gives grace to the humble." Therefore humble yourselves under the mighty hand of God, that He may exalt you in due time, casting all your care upon Him, for He cares for you. Be sober, be vigilant; because your adversary the devil walks about like a roaring lion, seeking whom he may devour. Resist him, steadfast in the faith, knowing that the same sufferings are experienced by your brotherhood in the world. (1 Peter 5:5–9)

Both James and Peter outlined a great strategy for us: humility can help us resist the Enemy's temptations so we don't fall into the world's trap. When we fully submit ourselves to God and cast all our cares and anxieties on Him, we are saying no to Satan and yes to God. Both James and Peter gave us this same directive: submit and resist!

The apostle John added, "This is the victory that has overcome the world—our faith" (1 John 5:4). So it seems that a combination of humility and faith in the One who has already "overcome the world" (John 16:33) brings us victory over Satan and the attractions of the worldly domain he oversees.

Battle Strategy: Humility will please the Lord and vanquish the Enemy. Be humble before God and in all your relationships. How do you do that? Our Commander says to turn the other cheek, love and pray for our enemies, go the extra mile, give to him who asks you (Matthew 5:39, 41, 42, 44). Humbly love and serve God and His people. He will, in turn, exalt you above the battle.

THE FLESH

Our third enemy is "the flesh," a term the Bible uses to refer to the sinful or fallen nature we are all born with. Our flesh is always trying to lead us into sin and overindulgence; the Spirit, on the other hand, is trying to lead us toward a life of holiness and self-control. It is an internal war. The flesh desires pleasure and wants to be gratified and satisfied at any cost. It will entice us to make an idol out of just about everything: sex, money, television, the Internet, music, food—you name it. Now there is nothing wrong with any of those things unless they lead us into sin (sexual sin/pornography, the love of money, overeating, etc.) or we allow them to control us, for then they hinder our walk with God.

Paul described this internal battle in Romans 7:

> "I know that in me (that is in my flesh) nothing good dwells;
> for to will is present with me, but *how* to perform what is good
> I do not find. For the good I will to do, I do not do; but the evil
> I will not to do, that I practice." (vv. 18–19)

Can you relate? The flesh will entice us to retaliate instead of humbly seeking a peaceful resolution, pick up the remote instead of picking up the phone to call a friend in need, open a web browser instead of opening the Bible—you get the picture.

The flesh and the Holy Spirit are literally at war within us, and one of them is going to win every time:

> The flesh lusts against the Spirit, and the Spirit against the
> flesh; and these are contrary to one another, so that you do not
> do the things you wish. (Galatians 5:17)

The flesh opposes everything our spiritual nature encourages us to do. The war rages within us, and we must conquer our flesh. Hear Paul's answer for dealing with the flesh:

> Walk in the Spirit, and you shall not fulfill the lust of the flesh.... Those who are Christ's have crucified the flesh with its passions and desires. If we live in the Spirit, let us also walk in the Spirit. (Galatians 5:21, 24–25)

In prayer, we crucify our flesh each day by humbly submitting to God and choosing to rely on His Spirit's strength for victory over the works of the flesh (see Galatians 5:18–21). Below is the benchmark for knowing who's winning the battle against the flesh. Are these traits increasing in your life?

> The fruit of the Spirit is love, joy, peace, longsuffering, kindness, goodness, faithfulness, gentleness, self-control. (Galatians 5:22)

Another powerful way of dealing with the flesh is to deny it, and we do that by fasting and praying. When Jesus overcame Satan's temptations in the wilderness, He had been fasting. So when you are under attack or just can't seem to get your flesh under control, stop feeding it and feast on God's Word instead.

Before we move on from this discussion, I want to share with you my routine for my daily battle with the world and the flesh. You may find it helpful.

1. Each morning I give God the first moments of my day. When I open my eyes, I do what Joshua did: I "choose for [myself] this day whom [I] will serve" (Joshua 24:15). I say, "Good morning, Lord! I love You, and I choose to serve You today."

2. I go to my secret place (the extra room in our house) and shut the door. (If you have to grab a cup of coffee first, do it!)

3. I turn on a favorite worship song and center my mind on Christ. Of course my mind is already wanting to run in different directions, so as I sing, I focus on the words and wholeheartedly worship my King.

4. I get on my knees and pray a simple prayer: "Lord Jesus, help me live today with You as my Lord.... I surrender to You my heart, my mind, and my day.... I crucify my flesh (Galatians 2:20) and offer my body as a living sacrifice (Romans 12:1).... Holy Spirit, fill me with Your love and power (Luke 11:13)." Then I put on the full armor (see Ephesians 6:10–17; more about this in chapter 8)

5. I ask the Lord if there is anything He wants to say to me and sit quietly for a little while to listen.

6. I pick up my Bible and read out loud a psalm or a chapter so that I hear the truth as well as see it.

7. Then I take a few more minutes to pray for those I am warring for. If I am in the midst of a particularly difficult battle, I may fast from breakfast and spend that time praying.

I know these seven steps might look a little daunting, but all seven can be done in fifteen or twenty minutes. Make time! A few moments in the Lord's presence each morning can set the trajectory of your whole day heavenward. Try my approach, tweak it, or come up with a routine that works for you. Do something! Every one of us warriors needs to find ways to resist the pull of the world and the flesh.

As long as we remain in these bodies of flesh, we will continue to battle the evil three. But we can be strong in the Lord's mighty power, enabled by Him to fight the good fight each day. After all, we have been crucified with Christ and raised to a new life. And right now we are about to discover just how high He has lifted us.

VICTORY SEAT

[God] raised us up together, and made us sit together
in the heavenly places in Christ Jesus.
EPHESIANS 2:6

The verse you just read is a game changer. Read it one more time.

I spent most of my Christian life focused on the Cross, as we believers should, but that moment signifies just the beginning of the Good News. There is so much more to our faith beyond the Cross!

After all, having been resurrected from the dead, Jesus ascended into heaven where He sits at the right hand of God, ruling and reigning over the whole universe. Being at God's right hand is a way of saying He is in a place of divine authority. Just before His ascension, Jesus proclaimed to His disciples, "All authority has been given to Me in heaven and on earth" (Matthew 28:18). Having accomplished His mission on earth, Warrior Jesus had taken His rightful place on the throne of heaven where He continues to reign over all physical and spiritual realms. (This is why we pray "in Jesus' name": He has all authority in every realm.) But, amazingly, the story continues with—according to Ephesians 2:6— God raising *us* up far above all the forces of evil and seating *us* next to Christ. In the spiritual realm, we are at this very moment at the right hand of God, sharing in Christ's authority. A pivotal change has taken place: we find ourselves in a position of victory and—as we do battle in prayer—we will be more effective if we know, understand, and act according to the power and authority God has given us.

In *The Invisible War*, pastor and writer Chip Ingram says, "We are not fighting *for* victory, but *from* victory." That sentence revolutionized the battle for me. You and I are sitting together with Christ, right now, above all evil powers. Paul said *together* three times in Ephesians 2:5–

6, emphasizing the unconquerable power that comes with our unity as Christ's army. We can stand confidently against our enemies from this place of victory, far above all principalities, powers, rulers, and spiritual forces of wickedness, as Paul described in Ephesians 6.

So being seated with Christ is a huge factor in our advancing in the battle. We are seated in a place of authority with our King, a place that is also a position of rest. We can be at peace in the fiercest storms because we are *seated* with our Commander above the fray. I know these ideas may sound new and strange, but they are simply the truth. And knowing and applying the truth—all of God's truth—gives us a great advantage in the spiritual war.

God Himself says we are seated with Christ in the heavenly realms, and we know God does not lie. So our heavenly seat with Christ is our position in the battle. Christ reigns victorious, and we are called to be His already-victorious warriors on earth, already ruling and reigning with Him:

> Those who receive abundance of grace and of the gift of righteousness will reign in life through the One, Jesus Christ. (Romans 5:17)

If we incorporate these truths into our prayer life as well as our daily walk with God, our battle against the world, the flesh, and the Devil will be very different. Sitting next to the Commander in Chief, who has a bird's-eye view of the whole battlefield, is a tremendous advantage. After all, any good Commander points out the danger zones and landmines in His soldiers' path. Jesus knows every clever device, cunning trick, and wicked scheme of the Enemy *before* they unfold or are activated. Of course He will reveal that intel to His good soldiers so we will know how to pray. Hear Jesus' promise:

> "When He, the Spirit of truth, has come, He will guide you into all truth; for He will not speak on His own authority, but

whatever He hears He will speak; and He will tell you things to come." (John 16:13)

Again, what an advantage in battle!

Remember when the king of Syria was warring against Israel, but every battle move he tried was somehow being made known to his opponents? The king was greatly distressed and suspected treason. Finally, he said to his servants, "Will you not show me which of us is for the king of Israel?" And one of the servants said, "None, my lord, O king; but Elisha, the prophet who is in Israel, tells the king of Israel the words that you speak in your bedroom" (2 Kings 6:11–12). Jesus, the Commander of heaven's armies, was telling Elisha exactly what Israel's military enemy was going to do before they did it.

Now I'm not saying we will get to know everything ahead of time, but I am saying that the more tuned in we are to Christ's voice, the more often and more easily we can thwart the Enemy's covert operations and sneak attacks. Granted, sometimes we will experience God letting us go right into the heat of battle without warning. But if we are grounded in the truth that our Commander is in complete control of the whole war, we can know His peace. A battle may seem out of control, but we can be certain that it is unfolding exactly as the Commander wills. Nothing takes Him by surprise, and nothing can alter His plan. That fact gives me great confidence about fighting the good fight for Christ on any battlefield He chooses to send me. From the victory seat of God-given authority, we fight this war with help from our Commander. Day by day and in His strength, we destroy Enemy strongholds, take back land, and advance the kingdom.

EXTRAVAGANT GRACE

By grace you have been saved [sozo] through faith,
and that not of yourselves, it is the gift of God.
EPHESIANS 2:8

Grace may be difficult to adequately define, and before we start trying to define it, know this: grace is everything we need. Furthermore, every gift, every blessing, every wonderful thing God has done for us, especially our salvation—it's all grace.

God's grace is amazing. I have humbly sung that truth many times, and I still marvel that God could be so gracious and merciful to me, as sinful and rebellious as I was. I will also never understand how He could watch His Son suffer the brutal abuse and an excruciatingly painful death by crucifixion in order to pay my debt, but God the Father watched as Jesus the Son did exactly that. This acrostic for the word *grace* captures that meaning:

GOD'S RICHES AT CHRIST'S EXPENSE

Our God is full of grace and mercy, and that truth alone is reason enough to thank Him and praise Him for the rest of our days!

God's grace is abundant. Lately, I find myself praying almost constantly, "God, give me the grace I need for what I am about to do." I may be leading worship, running a meeting at work, or simply talking with my wife or daughter. Whatever I do, I know I need more grace. I'm guessing you do too. So before you go into any situation, pause for a moment and humbly ask God to give you the grace you need. I love this declaration of God's extravagant grace:

> God is able to make all grace abound toward you, that you, always having all sufficiency in all things, may have an abundance for every good work. (2 Corinthians 9:8)

God's grace is unmerited. We can't earn God's grace, and we definitely don't deserve it, but because of His great love for us, we reap all the benefits of His grace. However great the depths of our sin, God's grace can reach into the pit, pull us out, clean us up, and get us back on the warrior path. Charles Spurgeon, a nineteenth-century pastor and writer, said this:

> The bridge of grace will bear your weight, brother. Thousands of big sinners have gone across that bridge, yea, tens of thousands have gone over it. Some have been the chief of sinners and some have come at the very last of their days but the arch has never yielded beneath their weight. I will go with them trusting to the same support. It will bear me over as it has for them.

Amen to that! God's grace covers the believer who has followed Christ from childhood as well as the thief on the cross next to Jesus who made a last-minute, eternity-changing decision. And that thief ate from the Tree of Life in paradise that same day. It was grace.

God's grace shows His favor. Whether we realize it or not, we are constantly blessed and protected by God's unearned, undeserved favor. At times, when there was truly no explanation for what happened other than God's goodness toward me, I have been astounded by His favor. I have received bonuses when I was broke, promotions at work I never asked for, resolutions to conflicts that seemed at an impasse—all evidence of my heavenly Father's unceasing favor. A friend's daughter called this "mad favor" when she saw the incredible things God was doing in her life. What a great way of describing God's grace. Because of His unconditional love and unchanging faithfulness, He shows us mad favor!

God's grace is merciful. Whatever we are facing, we can boldly approach His throne and find the grace we need at the very moment we need it. Be it peace, healing, strength, financial help, forgiveness, or something else, Jesus said, "Ask, and it will be given to you; seek, and you will find; knock, and it will be opened to you" (Matthew 7:7). God's throne of grace is always approachable:

> Let us therefore come boldly to the throne of grace, that we may obtain mercy and find grace to help in time of need. (Hebrews 4:16)

God's grace is powerful. When Paul was suffering from the thorn in his side and asked God to remove it, the Almighty's answer was... grace: "My grace is sufficient for you, for my power [*dunamis*] is made perfect in weakness" (2 Corinthians 12:9 NIV). God didn't deliver Paul from his affliction; He wanted Paul to trust that His grace would provide more than enough power to sustain him in his pain and suffering. Jack Hayford says this:

> [God's] grace is powerful and all-enabling to the believer. His grace facilitates our abilities to conquer every weakness as we yield to an absolute trust or reliance upon God, trusting His heart even when we cannot trace His hand. [2]

The Greek words for *gifts* and *grace* are nearly the same—*charisma* and *charis*, respectively. So the gifts of the Holy Spirit are given, by grace, so that you and I are able to minister to those people around us as the Spirit wills. God's grace not only covers all our weaknesses and sin, but it allows us to share in the Lord's power so we can do ministry effectively.

God's supply of grace is unlimited. Don't hesitate to ask Him for more. And remember, when the battle is raging around you, His grace will surround you.

> **Battle Strategy:** Thank God daily—even several times a day—for His grace and mercy. Go boldly before His throne for whatever you need and as often as you need to. His grace will sustain you.

GOD'S SONG

*We are [God's] workmanship, created in Christ
Jesus for good works, which God prepared
beforehand that we should walk in them.*
EPHESIANS 2:10

I love the craft of songwriting. There is something ethereal about pulling melodies and lyrics, seemingly from thin air, and fusing them together into a four- or five-minute musical experience. I can never go too long without sitting down with my guitar and engaging in that creative process. For me, the process usually starts with a melody for a single simple line that will be part of the chorus, and as I strum my guitar, words and ideas start to flow. I keep going back over it, honing every word, sculpting and crafting each line, until I feel it is exactly the way it should be. Granted, sometimes the results are less than wonderful, but every now and then—by God's grace!—the melody and words seem to blend together seamlessly, perfectly. I play the new song over and over, finding great pleasure in this new creation that I breathed life into from inception to completion.

God, on the other hand, never writes a bad song, and He has penned quite a few. Trillions, actually. You see, we are His songs, the masterwork of His hands. The Greek word for *workmanship* (Ephesians 2:10) is *poiema*, which is the source of our word *poem*. So God, the master Wordsmith, creates each of His precious songs with an incredible storyline from start to finish. Madly in love with and fiercely committed to each one He creates, God then weaves His songs together like a musical tapestry.

Thousands of years ago, our loving and creative God started writing glorious songs. Unfortunately, not everyone likes God's taste in music. In fact, the Enemy despises every song God writes, so he does his best to stop the music. Our Enemy can't succeed unless we let him. And why would you let him when God has written your song, and no one else can sing it like you can? You are a masterpiece written by God's own hand. Don't let your song go unsung. Sing it as an anthem of praise to your gracious God!

BLOOD COVERED

Precious blood by this we conquer in the fiercest fight,
Sin and Satan overcoming by its might.

F. R. HAVERGAL

*Now in Christ Jesus you who once were far off have been brought
near by the blood of Christ. For He Himself is our peace.*
EPHESIANS 2:13–14

Jesus' blood is a crucial weapon in spiritual warfare. The blood of Christ washes away all of our sin and is therefore one of our most powerful weapons because it answers every accusation of the Enemy. Whatever charge he brings against us, the verdict is "not guilty" because we are in Christ, forgiven, and washed clean.

Before I gave my life to Christ, Satan could have accused me of just about anything, and he had every right to do so. I was guilty of it all. But the cross of Calvary was my watershed, and the moment I accepted Christ as my Savior, I received my acquittal. I was fully pardoned, and Satan lost all grounds for any accusations. I was set free and brought near to God by Jesus' shed blood.

Revelation 12:11 says, "[We] overcame [the accuser] by the blood of the Lamb and by the word of [our] testimony" (Revelation 12:11). We need to proclaim out loud to Satan that the blood of the Lamb has cleansed us of our sins, enabled us to be in relationship with God, and opened the door to an eternity with Him in heaven. We need to testify to our Enemy that we have been completely forgiven of our sins. When the Enemy brings a false accusation against me, I remind him that I am in Christ—forgiven and washed clean by His blood—so all his accusations are empty. The confession of our faith in the power of the blood is essential to our maintaining victory over the Evil One. In *Overcoming the Enemy*, Charles Stanley wrote, "When we engage in spiritual warfare against the devil, we are wise to pray, 'By the authority of Jesus Christ and under the protection of His shed blood, I pray against you, Satan.'"[3]

The blood of Jesus washes away our sin (1 John 1:7) and brings us peace with our holy God (Colossians 1:20). Jesus' blood cleanses our souls of guilt (Hebrews 9:14) and allows us entrance into the most holy place, God's very presence (Hebrews 10:19–21). And Jesus' blood sanctifies us (Hebrews 13:12), purifies us (Ezekiel 43:20), and gives us abundant life (John 6:53). There is incredible life and power in Jesus' blood.

You have been brought near to God, warrior, but the Accuser is near you as well. So stay close to Jesus. Stockpile in your arsenal Revelation 12:11 and other verses about Jesus' cleansing blood and use them for your protection. When you are under attack, remind yourself—and remind Satan—that Christ's blood has washed you clean. You are forgiven and free—and the Enemy knows it. Make it your mission to see that he doesn't forget!

Battle Strategy: Daily when you pray, ask Jesus to protect your family, yourself, and your entire domain (your home, property, possessions, and sphere of influence) with His blood. Wield the truth about the power of Jesus' blood as a weapon to defuse the Enemy's accusations (see also "The Blood of Jesus" in chapter 10).

THE CORNERSTONE

You are... members of the household of God, having been
built on the foundation of the apostles and prophets, Jesus
Christ Himself being the chief cornerstone, in whom the
whole building, being fitted together, grows into a holy
temple in the Lord, in whom you also are being built
together as a dwelling place of God in the Spirit.
EPHESIANS 2:19–22

In construction, first the cornerstone is set; only then can a solid foundation be built. Over time, a building will stand or fall based on how strong its foundation was. And we are laying a foundation in these first three chapters of Ephesians so we can stand firm and strong.

Spiritually speaking, Christ is the foundation, the solid Rock, on which we build our lives if we are wise (Matthew 7:24–25). When you regularly read the Word of God and walk in intimate fellowship with Him, you give the Master Builder raw materials with which to construct your life. Brick by brick, He enables you to raise up solid walls that rest upon the solid Rock. Every spiritual blessing, every word of wisdom and revelation, every gift, lesson, trial, and victory— each is another brick in the wall, and when we trust God, He uses our faith as the mortar.

The Ephesians 2 passage above is actually talking about Christ being the cornerstone of the church, and none of us will be effective in the church if we as individuals are not standing strong on who we are in Christ.

One morning when I was reading my Bible, the passage below leaped off the page at me:

> Do you not know that your body is the temple of the Holy Spirit who is in you, whom you have from God, and you are not your own? For you were bought at a price; therefore glorify God in your body and in your spirit, which are God's. (1 Corinthians 6:19–20)

Up to that moment, I had considered my body my own, and here God let me know otherwise! This fact put Romans 12:1—"present your bodies a living sacrifice, holy, acceptable to God"—in a new light. I realized the radical truth that our bodies are temples and that, like the Old Testament tabernacle, God's presence dwells inside.

After the incredible temple in Jerusalem was complete, King Solomon dedicated it to God with worship and prayer. After Solomon prayed, God showed the people how immensely pleased He was:

> When Solomon finished praying, fire flashed down from heaven and burned up the burnt offerings and sacrifices, and

the glorious presence of the LORD filled the Temple. The priests could not enter the Temple of the LORD because the glorious presence of the LORD filled it. When all the people of Israel saw the fire coming down and the glorious presence of the LORD filling the temple, they fell face down on the ground and worshiped and praised the LORD. (2 Chronicles 7:1–3 NLT)

Can you imagine seeing fire come down from the sky and the presence of God fill the temple like a cloud? No wonder the people fell face down in awe! For us, this Old Testament scene foreshadowed the Holy Spirit filling our physical body, referred to as a temple in 1 Corinthians 6:19–20. We are now—each one of us—a temple of the living God. His plan always was to fill us with His glorious presence—with His Holy Spirit—so that, collectively, we can be the powerhouse church He intends us to be, His church that will share His gospel and change the world.

Maybe today, then, we need to have our own dedication ceremony. Let's consecrate our temples to God, make Him the Cornerstone of our lives, and proclaim that we will build our lives on Christ the Solid Rock and on Him alone! May His presence fill you so mightily that you, too, will fall face down in worship!

THE TAKEAWAY

As a warrior in Christ, I declare that ...

- I was dead in my sin but have been made alive (Ephesians 2:1).
- I will submit to God and resist the devil, the world, and the flesh (2:2–3).
- I have been raised up and seated with Jesus in a position of authority far above my enemies (2:6).
- I am saved by grace through faith: salvation is God's gift to me (2:8).
- I am God's masterpiece, and He has written a good plan for my life (2:10).
- I have been reconciled to God and brought near to Him by Christ's blood (2:13).
- I have the peace of God in my heart, for Christ is my peace (2:14).
- I am God's temple, and Christ is my Cornerstone (2:20).
- I am being built into a dwelling place of God by the Spirit (2:21–22).

Heavenly Father, thank You for the Cross, for Your victory over sin and death, for raising me from the dead, and giving me new life in Christ. I am crucified with Christ, and I no longer live but Christ lives in me. I renounce all agreements I have made with the world, my flesh, and the Enemy. Empower me by Your Spirit to overcome these enemies of my soul. Thank You for seating me with Christ in a position of victory and for Your precious blood that has reconciled me to You and allows me to walk in Your peace. Jesus, I pray the protective covering of Your blood over my family, my home, and all of my domain today. You alone are the Cornerstone of my faith and the Rock on which I stand. I surrender my life to You today, for Your purposes and glory. In Jesus' name I pray. Amen.

WAR ROOM DISCUSSION

1. The world, the flesh, and the devil are enemies of a warrior's soul. Why does humility enable us to stand strong against the temptations the world offers?

2. To crucify our fleshly desires, we need to "walk in the Spirit." What does that look like? Be specific.

3. What power has God's grace given you perhaps for a specific season, for a thorn in your side, or for a stressful situation? Give Him glory as you reflect on that experience of His goodness, His faithfulness, and His grace.

4. What impact can knowing you are God's masterpiece have on your everyday life? on your self-talk? on your relationships with people? on your relationship with Him?

5. What does it mean to plead the blood of Christ over your life—over your spouse, family, work, or ministry?

READ EPHESIANS 3

5

AUTHORIZED
POWER AND PURPOSE

All authority comes from God.
ROMANS 13:1

Authorize: to give power or permission to:
to give legal or official approval[1]

My last management job began with my being handed the most challenging group of people I had ever encountered. I was to supervise these forty wonderful but diverse employees. I'm not sure how many languages were represented, but the Tower of Babel comes to mind. Just as in that Bible story, there was much confusion. In addition, many of the people didn't see eye to eye—on anything. I inherited multiple problems that had never been dealt with, and to top it off, the forty of them were out to test the new guy.

I remember one particular meeting early on when the natives were getting restless and a little out of hand. I don't remember the specifics, but I do remember rumblings of discontent as I tried to conduct the meeting. That's when a Vietnamese woman stood up and cried out, "We need you to be strong and lead us!" *Gulp.* I will never forget that moment. Then and there I realized that people needed me to step up, be strong, and walk in my authority for the good of everyone.

God's call to the spiritual warrior is the same: "I need you to be strong and lead!"

God needs warriors.

Like no other book in the Bible, Ephesians reveals how God put everything, in every realm, under the unconquerable authority of Christ. Jesus died on the cross, was raised in power, and ascended to the right hand of God where He was given total authority over all powers, both good and evil (see Ephesians 1:21–23). Our being seated with God means He is now sharing that authority with us. Simply put, *authority* is "delegated power," and the Almighty God has delegated incredible power to us. If you are like me, you have probably walked around somewhat unaware of the matchless power and authority God has given you in Christ. It is part of the inheritance of every Christ-follower. We have been authorized to do on earth what God wills to be done from heaven, and we have His delegated authority to accomplish our mission.

BEHIND ENEMY LINES

We find confirmation of this delegated authority in an amazing report in Luke 10. Having already sent out the twelve apostles (Luke 9:1), our Commander summoned seventy other trained disciples and briefed them on a special ops mission: He was sending them out to invade Enemy territory (Luke 10:1–16). And Jesus "sent them two by two before His face into every city and place where He Himself was about to go" (v. 1). Jesus instructed them to heal the sick and announce the coming of God's kingdom (v. 9).

Then, according to Luke, "The seventy returned with joy, saying, 'Lord, even the demons are subject to us in your name'" (v. 17). Notice that the only ministry they mention is the authority they were able to wield against Satan's army. Jesus joyfully replied, "I saw Satan fall like lightning from heaven" (v. 18). Jesus confirmed that He had given them power and authority and that they had used it successfully on their mission. Satan and the kingdom of darkness took a mighty blow at the hands of seventy unnamed but faithful and bold warriors.

Jesus then proclaimed these game-changing words: "Behold, I have given you the authority to trample on serpents and scorpions, and over all the power of the enemy, and nothing shall by any means hurt you" (v. 19). Jesus was not talking about actual snakes and scorpions here, but about Satan and his evil emissaries as well as the power our Lord gives us to overcome them.

Jesus went on to tell the seventy, "Do not rejoice in this, that the spirits are subject to you, but rather rejoice because your names are written in heaven" (v. 20). Jesus confirmed that the disciples would defeat demons, but the fact that their names were written in the Book of Life for eternity was to be for them a greater cause for celebration.

Continuing the story, Luke wrote, "In that hour Jesus rejoiced in the Spirit and said, 'I thank You, Father, Lord of heaven and earth, that You have hidden these things from the wise and prudent and revealed them to babes'" (v. 21). This verse is key to why the disciples' mission was so successful. The seventy apparently had *childlike faith and trust in Jesus*—unlike the religious leaders of their time—so they believed Jesus and were able to do what He said they could do. So seventy ordinary Christ-following men—just like you and me—changed the world and rocked the heavenly realms.

The Word of God says we have power and authority *in Christ* to do what these seventy did: we, too, can preach the gospel boldly, heal the sick, and cast out demons. Look at what the psalmist said about the authority we can exercise in warfare in order to conquer our enemies: "Let the high praises of God be in their mouth, and a two-edged sword in their hand, to execute vengeance on the nations, and punishments on the peoples; *to bind their kings with chains, and their nobles with fetters of iron*; to execute on them the written judgment—*this honor have all his saints*" (Psalm 149:6–9, emphasis added). "All his saints" includes you and me, meaning that the psalmist's words apply to the spiritual war you and I are fighting today.

So I take Jesus at His word that we have authority over demons, but I must say I have very little expertise in the area of casting them out of someone. What I would say is, I have stood strong in prayer for my wife, friends, family, and myself and, like the seventy, have experienced the victory of making the Enemy flee. I have spoken the Word of God at him, commanded him in Jesus' name to go, and witnessed chaotic situations turn into God encounters. I have turned to worship as a means of warfare, and as the praises of God have come out of my mouth, I have felt oppression and fear scattering and God's peace enveloping my heart and filling the room. And all His saints can exercise their God-given authority over demons and experience this same kind of victory.

Jesus has authorized us to wield His power and authority, according to His will, as we join Him in the spiritual war against the forces of evil in our world. It does, however, require childlike faith and dependence on God. The more complete our surrender to Christ, the greater His strength in us becomes, enabling us to win the battles we all must face.

In Christ, we have warrior authority!

THE FORGOTTEN MYSTERY

He made known to me the mystery.
EPHESIANS 3:3

I was chosen to explain to everyone this mysterious plan that God, the Creator of all things, had kept secret from the beginning.
EPHESIANS 3:9 NLT

The apostle Paul was a warrior on a mission. His assignment was to unveil our new position in Christ and reveal the great "mystery" that God had hidden since the beginning of the ages. The mystery was God's intent to unite Gentiles and Jews as one body, His church; raise it up with the Head, Jesus Christ; and bestow on it all authority to rule and reign with Him. The secret was out: the church of Christ followers was created to be a powerhouse on earth, partnering with

God for the advance of the kingdom. Fiercely dedicated to this mission, Paul endured shipwrecks, beatings, and imprisonments, but nothing stopped him from revealing the astounding good news (see 2 Corinthians 11:22–28). Paul was a dedicated warrior committed to an eternal cause.

Sadly, I believe some aspects of the mystery that Paul laid down his life to reveal have nearly been lost over time. For instance, I was a Christian for many years before I ever heard it said that Christ's church is to be a united, powerful force exercising authority over the forces of evil in the heavenly realms. Why isn't this message proclaimed—and proclaimed loudly? Fear, for one thing. I think many church leaders fear they will lose credibility and members if they spend much time talking about invisible realms and unseen wars. Also, we have an Enemy whose strategy involves dividing and conquering: when we are divided, we have very little power. The Enemy goes to great lengths to keep us either sleeping on our watch or warring with each other. We are supposed to be warriors, united in our cause and raised up together as a mighty army equipped to carry the truth to a lost and dying world and to undo the works of the Enemy. If we could wake up enough to get our faith behind these truths about the power we have in Christ, together we could change the world. If we really understood the power that the church has been given in Christ, we would see multitudes turn from darkness to light. Acting as God's hands and feet on this earth, we are to shine His light to the whole cosmos:

> God's purpose . . . was to use the church to display his wisdom in its rich variety to all the unseen rulers and authorities in the heavenly places. This was his eternal plan, which he carried out through Christ Jesus our Lord. (Ephesians 3:10–11 NLT)

No wonder Paul had to deal with so much resistance and opposition! Satan had to work hard to try to keep Paul from waking people up to an understanding of God's full plan and intent for His church.

Paul dedicated his life to proclaiming the gospel and preparing warriors for the battle. Because of that, the Enemy attacked fiercely and often, so Paul's life was fraught with difficulty and challenges. Yet God was with this tenacious warrior, strengthening and guiding him through every trial and storm. Paul was a warrior with a purpose, and like a champion he ran his race to the finish line. We may not be called to endure the many hardships that he did, but we are all called to understand and reveal the great mystery.

EVERY WARRIOR'S MISSION

I became a minister according to the gift of the grace of
God given to me by the effective working of His power.
EPHESIANS 3:7

As he reflected on his life, Paul credited the good he was able to do to God's grace and Christ's power that were working mightily in him and through him. In Ephesians 3:7, the word *working* means "energy." Jesus Christ, by grace, was energizing Paul so he could complete his mission. Paul had an incredible calling on his life, and relying on God's power, Paul stepped up and answered the call.

If we are honest with ourselves, we all desperately want to believe we have a great purpose for being on this planet, a mission worth laying down our lives for. So using words spoken by Nehemiah, let me set forth at least part of that purpose. His empowering words might even become part of your personal mission statement:

Don't be afraid of the enemy! Remember the Lord, who is great and glorious, and fight for your brothers, your sons, your daughters, your wives, and your homes! (Nehemiah 4:14 NLT)

Those words about our noble cause and mission are as compelling today as the day they were uttered. Consider the three main points

Nehemiah made here: 1) Don't fear the Enemy; 2) Give God glorious praise; and 3) Fight in defense of the people God puts on your path. Jesus lived according to these principles every day of His life as He fulfilled His mission on earth. Jesus not only fearlessly faced His enemies, but He also glorified God by both fighting for and serving the people around Him.

Day by day Jesus was on a mission *for* His Father and *with* His Father. Jesus Himself said, "The Son can do nothing of Himself, but what He sees the Father do" (John 5:19). Often Jesus went to solitary places to pray (see Mark 1:35), and in those moments of communing with His Father, Jesus received His marching orders and got recharged with divine power. In one instance, Jesus went out in the wilderness and prayed the entire night. In the morning He chose His twelve apostles (see Luke 6:12–16), then went down the mountain and healed a multitude: "for power went out from Him and healed them all" (Luke 6:19). All in a day's work!

Studying the life of Joshua recently, I came across this verse in Exodus that explains, at least in part, why God called Joshua to lead His people:

> So the LORD spoke to Moses face to face, as a man speaks to his friend. And he would return to the camp, but his servant Joshua the son of Nun, a young man, did not depart from the tabernacle. (Exodus 33:11)

As a young man, Joshua never departed from the Lord's presence. Even when Moses went back to camp, Joshua stayed in the tabernacle to commune with his heavenly Father. No wonder God chose him to take over for Moses and lead the conquest of the Promised Land: Joshua loved God and was sold out for God's purposes. The secret weapon of every warrior is to love God and stay close to Him. In the shelter of His wings, He will protect us and guide us on the path. The only times Joshua faltered after becoming Israel's leader was when he didn't ask God for direction (see Joshua 7:2–5 and Joshua 9), but that was rare. Joshua was a great leader and a mighty warrior because he stayed closely connected to the power source that made him great. Joshua took full advantage of the access he had to God, and we have that same access:

> In Christ Jesus our Lord... we have boldness and access with confidence through faith in Him. (Ephesians 3:11–12)

Joshua led the nation of Israel courageously, demonstrating the boldness and confidence that come only through time spent in the Lord's presence.

The Greek word for *boldness* is *parrhesia*, and it means "outspokenness, freedom of speech, candor, and cheerful courage."[5] *Parrhesia* enables ordinary people to act boldly with God-given authority and to exhibit the extraordinary power of the Holy Spirit as they—as we—serve God. We have this bold and confident access to God at all times because of Christ. With the full authority of heaven behind us and Christ living inside us, we can fearlessly advance on our mission with the boldness of a lion (Proverbs 28:1).

THE ULTIMATE BATTLE STANCE

For this reason I bow my knees to the
Father of our Lord Jesus Christ.
EPHESIANS 3:14

In abundant thankfulness for the mysteries God had revealed to him about our position in Christ ("for this reason"), Paul was humbly on his knees praying for both present and future warriors, asking God to grant them and us the power and authority needed for their divine mission. God has revealed the mystery, but the church can't carry out the mission without His power.

Though it seems totally illogical, a kneeling warrior is in the ultimate battle stance. This simple positional change can mean the difference between victory and defeat in a given situation. It's a position of total surrender to God. We never stand so strong against the Enemy as when we are bowed down before the King.

One night when I was upstairs writing, I heard a strange sound coming from downstairs. I went to investigate and found Cindy curled up on our bed sobbing. She had been experiencing a lot of spiritual attacks, and—without going into detail—this time the Enemy had fired an arrow the size of Texas at her. Because Cindy was already exhausted, the arrow had penetrated her armor, and she was ready to give up. I tried to comfort her and told her we needed to pray. She slid off the bed onto her knees, and I kneeled next to her. Done out of desperation, that prayer time on our knees was the turning point of the battle.

As we began and through tears, I asked the Lord to show me how we needed to pray. The Spirit immediately prompted me to start praising God. So I praised Him for His greatness, kindness, and mercy, and I started thanking Him for fighting for us. As I thanked Him more and more, verses of Scripture started coming to mind, so I started speaking them out loud. I proclaimed, "We are more than conquerors in Christ!" and "If God is for us, who can be against us!" and several others. I also pleaded the blood of Jesus over us and, in Jesus' name, told Satan and all of his emissaries that they had to flee.

When we finished praying, I could feel that a weight had lifted, and so could Cindy. The thick, dark heaviness that had been in the room moments earlier had been replaced by a sweet peace. Divine victory was in the air. As if those blessings weren't enough, God continued to teach us. Moments after we prayed, I picked up a devotional our church was reading together called *Draw the Circle* by Mark Batterson. In it, I read these words:

> There comes a moment when you must quit talking to God about the mountain in your life and start talking to the

mountain about your God. You proclaim His power. You declare His sovereignty. You affirm His faithfulness. You stand on His word. You cling to His promises.[2]

Mark then quotes five verses of Scripture on that page—the exact same five that the Spirit had just prompted me to pray! After that Mark ended the day's entry by saying, "When we hit our knees… that is where the battle is won and lost." Wow, minutes after the heat of battle, God recapped the whole event back to me in a book. That is the power of our God, and we tap more into that power when we are on our knees than we can anywhere else!

> **Battle Strategy:** Start your day on your knees, humbly before your King. Make it your ultimate battle stance!

THE MIGHTY RIVER

I pray that from his glorious, unlimited resources he will empower [dunamis] you with inner strength through his Spirit.
EPHESIANS 3:16 NLT

Ephesians 3:16 is one of my favorite verses in the Bible. Here, Paul prayed that our all-powerful, uncontainable God would, by His Spirit, infuse us with strength and power for our journey. Making this verse even more important to me, one day God gave me the picture of a three-part river running alongside the path of the warrior: this River, alive with power, represented the source from which we warriors draw our strength.

Before we get to this River, consider that water is made up of three parts: two atoms hydrogen and one atom oxygen. Similarly, I saw in my mind this River of God as also being comprised of three parts. God is the Fountainhead who pours out the three tributaries of power (*dunamis*), love (*agape*), and a sound mind (*sophronismos*): "God has not given us a spirit of fear, but of power and of love and of a sound mind" (2 Timothy 1:7). These three gifts from above are elements of a Mighty River that represents the Holy Spirit moving in our lives.

First of all, realize that the spirit of fear is one of the Enemy's favorite tools, and he uses it relentlessly. We all battle fear in some form, so there must be billions of "fear" spirits in Satan's army. I have battled fear most of my life, so I speak from experience. If you are walking in timidity or fear in any area of your life—and I know what that's like— you could be dealing with a spirit of fear. So let's examine the kind of power, love, and sound mind that, together, demolish the spirit of fear and allow us to walk in victory.

POWER AND LOVE

First, power. The word *empower* in Ephesians 3:16 and the word *power* in 2 Timothy 1:7 are both the Greek *power* word *dunamis*. As I described earlier, this is God's miracle-working power and strength that dwells inside us in the Person of the Holy Spirit.

Next, in 2 Timothy 1:7, *love* is not referring to romantic love. The Greek word for love in this verse is *agape,* and it is God's divine, unconditional love demonstrated in what Christ did for us on the cross. This second tributary of the River—God's ever-flowing, unfailing love for His people—becomes real in our lives through His Spirit. As Paul continued his prayer, he asked God to help us comprehend the magnitude of this love:

> Being rooted and grounded in love, may [you] be able to comprehend with all the saints what is the width and length and depth and height—to know the love of Christ which passes knowledge. (Ephesians 3:17–19)

In this very moment, Jesus Christ is residing and abiding in our hearts, and the River of His love is incomprehensibly wide and long and deep and high. The Nile River is a dried-up creek in comparison! Scripture says, "The love of God has been poured out in our hearts by the Holy Spirit who was given to us" (Romans 5:5 HCSB). So, speaking about fear, the Bible says this: "There is no fear in love; but perfect love casts out fear, because fear involves torment" (1 John 4:18). God let us know that His *agape* love removes all fear—and that He has a limitless amount of that love to give us.

Then, with a word picture that takes this river imagery a little further, Paul prayed in Ephesians 3:17 that we would be "rooted and grounded in love." First, we need to really know Christ's love. The word *know* means "to come to know" and "to become known."[1] Paul was talking about a deeply intimate relationship with Christ by which we become like mighty oak trees with our roots firmly established and well nourished by the River. This imagery is found in one of my favorite psalms:

> They delight in the law of the LORD,
> meditating on it day and night.
> They are like trees planted along the riverbank,
> bearing fruit each season.
> Their leaves never wither,
> and they prosper in all they do. (Psalm 1:2–3 NLT)

Ezekiel 47 also refers to fruit trees planted along the river and being nourished by it:

> Fruit trees of all kinds will grow along both sides of the river. The leaves of these trees will never turn brown and fall, and there will always be fruit on their branches. There will be a new crop every month, for they are watered by the river flowing from the temple. The fruit will be for food and the leaves for healing. (Ezekiel 47:12 NLT)

The power of the River flowing through us—of the Holy Spirit in us—will enable us to not only bear good fruit, but also should enable us to be a blessing to those around us. Our roots should be so deeply anchored in God's truth and the Holy Spirit's presence with us and within us that our lives are bearing beautiful fruit: "love, joy, peace, patience, kindness, goodness, faithfulness, gentleness, and self-control" (Galatians 5:22–23 NLT). Warriors filled with the Spirit and bearing good fruit will point people to Jesus.

MIND OF CHRIST

The third tributary of the River—the third aspect of the Holy Spirit—is a sound mind. As I mentioned, the Greek word here is *sophronismos.* I was amazed to discover that *sophron* means "saved or healed," and *phren* means "mind." So "sound mind" in 2 Timothy 1:7 means we have a saved or healed mind. Paul said it this way in 1 Corinthians 2: "We have the mind of Christ" (v. 16). We have peaceful, self-controlled minds when we walk in the power of the Spirit just as Jesus did.

For a picture of the difference between walking with and without the Holy Spirit, let's look at the life of Peter for a minute. The evening before Christ's arrest in the garden, Peter emphatically proclaimed to Jesus, "Even if I have to die with you I will never deny you!" (Matthew 26: 35 NLT). Unfortunately, the next day, Peter cursed and denied the Lord three times just as his Lord had predicted. Peter caved under the danger of being associated with Jesus because he had no power except his own. But after the Spirit is poured out fifty-two days later (Acts 2), we see that a major transformation took place. The fearful, Christ-denying Peter was now preaching a message that, by God's grace, saved three thousand people. After that, Peter walked to the temple to pray. Along the way Peter invoked the name of Jesus in faith and healed a man who had been crippled since birth.

What had happened to Peter? How did he go from powerless to powerful in such a short timespan? The answer is, the River was now flowing mightily through him. The Spirit of God, now living inside of Peter, gave him the audacious faith he needed to step out of his comfort zone and do whatever God called him to do. The power, love, and sound mind of the River now energized and guided him: Peter was walking the warrior path in the power of the Holy Spirit. The fearful man who had vehemently denied knowing Christ now couldn't stop talking about Him—even to the same men who had Jesus crucified. Peter was overflowing with the River, and its power made him fearless!

If we are not walking in the fullness of the Spirit, we are doomed to be like Peter before Pentecost—always trying to do the right thing in our own strength, but usually coming up short. Pre-Pentecost is where I spent most of my Christian life. This type of warrior, though well intentioned, will either quickly be taken out and lose hope or get sporadic victories and then retreat from weariness.

If you have ever experienced the power and love of the Holy Spirit flowing through you, I'm sure you would agree there is nothing else like it. No drug can compare (and I tried most of them) to the infusion of love, joy, and peace the fullness of the Spirit brings. God loves us completely, and He has poured out His love into us—rivers of it! The River fills us so full we can't help but overflow to those around us. Jesus taught this truth: "Whoever believes in me, as Scripture has said, rivers of living water will flow from within them. By this he meant the Spirit" (John 7:37–38 NIV).

When you combine the three components of the River, it is an un-conquerable combination:

Power enables us to live with strength and boldness as—granted authority by God—we do mighty works.

Love—God's *agape* love—casts out our fear and gives us courage to lay down our lives for others.

A sound mind keeps us in perfect peace no matter what we face.

LAY DOWN YOUR LIFE

The Holy Spirit, however, requires the ultimate sacrifice from us. Any soldier in an all-out war knows he could potentially lose his life at any moment. He is ready to lay it down for his family, his country, his beliefs, and his fellow warriors. Similarly, spiritual warriors need the Spirit to give us the courage to lay down our lives, deny ourselves, and take up our crosses daily (see Luke 9:23).

Peter denied Jesus, but he was not alone in his cowardice. Matthew 26:56 says, "All the disciples forsook Him and fled" (NLT). Even after spending three years with the Lord of the universe, the disciples were fearful. In addition, they still loved their own lives too much to lay them down as Jesus was about to lay down His. But power was coming, and on the day of Pentecost the Mighty River—the powerful Holy Spirit—was poured out, and the disciples became fearless warriors for the kingdom. The same can happen to us today when we pray for ourselves as Paul prayed for believers: "That you may be filled with all the fullness of God" (Ephesians 3:19). With the Mighty River's love and power flowing inside us, making us whole and holy, filling us "with all the fullness of God," we become the men of God that our Creator always meant us to be.

Going back to Ezekiel 47, I love the imagery in the prophet's vision. Ezekiel saw water flowing out from under the temple of the Lord, and the Lord walked him out about a hundred and fifty feet until the water came up to his ankles. Then the Lord measured out another one hundred and fifty feet, and the water was up to Ezekiel's knees, then up to his waist. Finally, the water was so deep Ezekiel couldn't cross it. This is a beautiful picture of walking in the Spirit. We should keep going deeper and deeper into the Mighty River.

What if we sought God first every morning and asked Him to fill us anew with the Mighty River? Imagine beginning the day by connecting with our King as the banks of the River overflow like the Jordan River in springtime. Throughout the day we draw power from the River—from the Spirit—and then pour the fruit of His presence in us out to the world around us. As the day goes on, we pray regularly and continually, stretching our roots deeper in order to draw more of the Living Water. When the end of the day approaches, the River is calm: it has done its job, providing strength to the mighty oaks throughout the day. The following day, with the rising of the sun, the process starts all over again. New day, new power!

What a waste to let the River flow by without drawing its strength into our roots. We need the power, love, and sound mind the Spirit provides us. His power flows freely for a purpose. Never hesitate to tap in.

> **Battle Strategy:** Pray daily for the Mighty River to fill you and flow freely through you to others. Then fearlessly pour God's love, joy, peace, patience, kindness, and goodness into the lives of those around you.

INFINITELY MORE

Now to Him who is able to do exceedingly abundantly above all we ask or think, according to the power that works in us, to Him be glory.
EPHESIANS 3:20-21

That verse is quite compelling, isn't it? Paul was saying that no matter what you or I can dream up and pray for, it will still fall pitifully short of what God can actually do. We serve a God who has absolutely no limits: He is all wise, all knowing, all loving, all powerful. So why do we play it safe? Why do we only attempt things we can pull off with little to no chance of failure? Because we are of little faith. God, however, gets greater glory from our lives when we step out of that safe place into the unknown where His limitless power and strength can be displayed before the world.

The truth is, we have an easier time accessing that power when we recognize how weak we are without Him. The more fully and frequently we rely on His power, the more glory He gets. First Corinthians 1:27 says, "God has chosen the foolish things of the world to put to shame the wise, and God has chosen the weak things of the world to put to shame the things which are mighty." I take great comfort in verses like that one. It reminds me that I don't have to be ashamed of my weaknesses and inadequacies. God can do His greatest work in weak, surrendered vessels. After all, we are the ones He chooses. So I stand in agreement with what Paul said:

> I am glad to boast about my weaknesses, so that the power of Christ can work through me. That's why I take pleasure in my weaknesses, and in the insults, hardships, persecutions, and troubles that I suffer for Christ. For when I am weak, then I am strong. (2 Corinthians 12:9–10 NLT)

True warriors walk in God's mighty power and strength. We have nothing to boast about except the incredible things God does for and through us, things exceedingly greater than we could ever imagine!

Battle Strategy: From time to time, pray the powerful prayers in Ephesians 1:15–23 and 3:14–21 for yourself and for those in your circle. Personalize these prayers by including the names of the people you are called to fight for.

THE STAND

In the first three chapters of Ephesians, Paul showed us that we have everything we need to stand strong in our faith. We understand that angel armies are warring for us and doing God's bidding to help us on our journey as we pray. We know we are saints in the kingdom of God: chosen, holy, blameless, adopted, accepted, forgiven, predestined, and sealed by the Holy Spirit. We are being rescued, restored, and renewed daily through salvation. By God's grace, we are completely forgiven for our sins and washed clean with the blood of Jesus. Our hearts have been awakened and strengthened by God's power. Our eyes are fully open to the spiritual realm and the invisible war raging around us. We glory in our position of authority, seated with Christ in the heavenly realms, far above our enemies. Finally, we have the Holy Spirit's power and love flowing through us, resulting in a sound mind that clearly hears the voice of our Commander King.

Standing on all of these facts will keep us on solid ground when opposition comes our way—and, trust me, opposition will come. But as battles rage, sometimes in rapid succession, the warrior will emerge, gaining confidence and strength with each victory he experiences in the power of the Spirit.

Now that we stand strong on the promises of who we are and what have in Christ, it's time we learn *the walk*.

THE TAKEAWAY

As a warrior in Christ, I declare that ...

- I am a member of His body (Ephesians 3:6).
- God has given me authority over all evil forces aligned against me (3:10).
- God is displaying His wisdom and power through me as a member of His church (3:10).
- I can boldly and confidently go before the throne of grace (3:12).
- the Mighty River—God's Holy Spirit—is flowing through me and empowering me for my mission (3:16).
- Jesus Himself dwells in my heart through faith (3:17)
- I am rooted and grounded in the love of Christ like a mighty oak tree at the side of a river (3:17–18).
- I am filled with all the fullness of life and power that comes from God (3:19).
- God's power within me can accomplish infinitely more than I can ever imagine (3:20).

Father, You have given all authority, power, dominion, and rule to Your Holy Son, Jesus. I humbly thank You for sharing that authority and power with me. Increase my belief in this truth, so I can be effective for Your kingdom today. Thank You, also, for revealing the mystery of Your incredible plan to me. I am blessed to be a part of Your powerful body, the church, and I pray for my local church as well as for the worldwide body of believers: raise us up together as a mighty army for You and for the advancement of Your kingdom. By Your Spirit strengthen me with power, love, and a sound mind. Help me to fully receive the extravagant love You have for me and to show that love to the people You place in my path today. In Jesus' name I pray. Amen.

WAR ROOM DISCUSSION

1. In Luke 10:19, Jesus stated, "I have given you authority over all the power of the enemy." (Note the metaphors Jesus used in the first part of that verse.) Why do you think the extent of a believer's power and authority is a well-kept secret?

2. We who are believers in Christ need to remember that Satan has no authority in our lives except what we give him or what God allows. In what ways do you and I give Satan authority over our lives?

3. In his book *Draw the Circle*, Mark Batterson wrote, "There comes a moment when you must quit talking to God about the mountain in your life and start talking to the mountain about your God." What mountain do you need to start talking to about your God? Take some time right now to do exactly that.

4. We human beings tend to like our safety and *not* like to address our weaknesses. Yet God's power and strength become evident when we step out in faith beyond our safe little worlds and despite our weakness. Who comes to mind as an example of stepping out of one's safety zone and glorifying God in what ensued? When have you experienced God's strength in your weakness? Be specific.

5. Reread out loud the first paragraph of "The Stand" *(it starts on page 105)* and replace every *we, our,* and *us* with *I, my,* and *me*. What details about this description *of yourself* stood out? Which were especially significant, striking, or empowering?

READ EPHESIANS 4

6

NEW

CALLING OUT THE WARRIOR

Calling: a strong inner impulse toward a particular course of action especially when accompanied by conviction of divine influence.[1]

I, therefore, the prisoner of the Lord, beseech you to walk worthy of the calling with which you were called.

EPHESIANS 4:1

I remember well the day my wife and I packed up everything we owned and moved to Nashville, hundreds of miles from the family we loved back in Ohio. I had become passionate about the craft of songwriting, and we initially moved so I could pursue that dream. Less than a year after the move, we discovered the real reason we went to Nashville: God wanted Cindy and me in His kingdom. He had to get me out of the bars I played in night after night in order to position us for the decision of a lifetime.

A woman whom Cindy worked with invited us to her church several times. Finally, on a sunny Sunday in 1998, we accepted her invitation. When the service started, the first thing that caught my attention was the music. The only church I had ever gone to as a boy had had a blue-haired lady playing a pipe organ—but this church was rocking! Full band. Great singers. Intimate worship. I had no clue people did church this way. I loved it!

The pastor delivered a great sermon that ended with a compelling altar call, the first one I had ever heard in person. He shared a beautiful presentation of the gospel and asked if anyone felt led to give his or her life to Christ. The Spirit of God was piercing my heart as he spoke. With tears streaming down my face, I wanted to leap out of my seat and run down that aisle—but I didn't. I left that day knowing I had missed the call.

Fortunately, that pastor showed up on our apartment doorstep a couple of days later and walked Cindy and me through Romans to help us understand salvation. When he finished, we were ready to turn our lives over to Jesus. The pastor led us to the Lord as we sat at our kitchen table on a cool spring evening in 1998. God is so good: He wouldn't give up on us. He led that pastor right to our door, and Cindy and I became new creations that night. I was thirty-five years old—and finally on the path.

A few years after my conversion, God repurposed my music and called me to start leading worship at the church I was attending. It was quite the transition from leading people in drunken sing-a-longs in the smoky bars of Columbus to leading people into the presence of God. But this was my true calling to music. More recently, God has been compelling me to reveal His warrior path to men I know. God is always calling His people to "carry out great exploits" that will build up and advance His kingdom (Daniel 11:32). If a task seems way out of your comfort zone, there's a good chance God is calling you to it.

In the first three chapters of Ephesians, Paul masterfully conveyed a myriad of incredible truths declaring who we are and what we possess in Christ. He built a solid foundation on which we now stand with Christ as the Cornerstone. Now in Ephesians 4:1 comes Paul's exhortation to us to "walk worthy of the calling" of God on our lives. One definition I found for "walk worthy" is "after a godly sort."[2] Christ is the ultimate "godly sort," so we listen for His call and follow where He leads. I have found that many times His calling comes through an invitation. Someone invited me to lead worship for a youth event—I accepted and the journey began. Someone invited me to Boot Camp—I accepted and my life was forever changed. What's really cool is that the Greek definition for *called* is "invitation"! God invites us into His glorious salvation story—and He doesn't write mediocre stories. Our Almighty God writes epic adventures! So we should always be anticipating His next invitation and, when it comes, be ready to step out and move forward on the path.

Jesus said, "Everyone who is of the truth hears my voice" (John 18:37). Listen for His voice and you will hear the call. Then start walking—and "walk worthy" after Jesus.

WARRIOR TRAITS

Be completely humble and gentle; be patient,
bearing with one another in love.
Make every effort to keep the unity of the
Spirit through the bond of peace.
EPHESIANS 4:2-3 NIV

I love God's timing....

Recently I was having a phone conversation that started going south, and so did my patience. Finally, done trying to reason with this person, I abruptly ended the call, confident that I had every right to handle it the way I did. Shortly afterward, I went up to my office and opened a devotional email headlined with Ephesians 4:2-3. Talk about conviction! Suddenly I didn't feel that I was so right. In fact, the Spirit let me know I had been downright rude and dismissive to this person.

Now think for a minute about the band of misfits whom Jesus dealt with on a daily basis. None of the disciples understood half of what He was trying to teach them. He had impetuous Peter, Thomas the doubter, Judas the thief—and all of them arguing about who was the greatest. They were a mess! But Jesus walked through life with them, patiently, lovingly, one step at a time—the same way He does with us.

Humble, gentle, patient, loving, peaceful—these aren't traits we immediately associate with a warrior, but that is exactly what they are. Correction: they are characteristics of a *Spirit-filled* warrior, and these traits are among the fruit of the Spirit listed in Galatians 5:22–23. Displaying these traits implies not weakness, but Spirit-empowered strength. Jesus was bold as a lion, but at the same time He lived out every one of the characteristics above.

To see these traits in action, just take the stairs to the upper room where the Son of God washed the feet of His closest followers (John 13:1–17). Enough said? Jesus showed us that humility is a huge component of the warrior's calling. He modeled for us how to love God by loving and serving God's people:

> If someone says, "I love God," and hates his brother, he is a liar; for he who does not love his brother whom he has seen, how can he love God whom he has not seen? And this commandment we have from Him: that he who loves God must love his brother also. (1 John 4:20–21)

South African pastor Andrew Murray (1828–1917) wrote this in his book *Humility*:

> It is easy to think we humble ourselves before God; humility towards men will be the only sufficient proof that our humility before God is real; that humility has taken up its abode in us; and become our very nature; that we actually, like Christ, have made ourselves of no reputation.[3]

Jesus' mission? Serve and give:

> "The Son of man did not come to be served, but to serve and to give His life a ransom for many." (Mark 10:45)

In sharp contrast to Jesus and the example He set for us, most of us warriors are used to striving to get, not give. Yet God calls us to a sacrificial, not a superficial life. So who has God placed in your life to serve in His name and with His grace? Your family and friends for sure, but look beyond that. And look closely. Hurting people are all around you. Some may look different from you. Others may get on your last nerve. Some may smell funny or seem like they are from another planet, yet God calls you and me to serve all these people and to try to make a difference in their lives.

> **Battle Strategy:** Ask God to increase the warrior traits in you daily. His Holy Spirit will enable you to live to love, live to serve, and live to give.

STRIKE UP THE BAND

Whether or not we men want to get together and share our needs, we clearly need to. Our collective pain over marital problems, job uncertainties, confusion in fathering, self-doubts and the like, cries out for an audience of fellow men—brothers in both suffering and hope, fellow soldiers battling together after victory.
GORDON DALBEY[4]

Make every effort to keep yourselves united in the Spirit.
EPHESIANS 4:3 NLT

Misdirected as I was, I loved playing in bands growing up, and I still love being a part of the worship team at church on Sundays. Each member brings his or her particular musical talent to the group and, collectively, these gifts blend into one (hopefully) joyful and beautiful sound. When all the individual members know their instrument and their part in the song, the outcome can be so powerful.

A band of musicians is a great analogy for what God can do with a unified group of believers. In God's band each one of us has an integral part to play, and He wants each of us to bring our best to the ensemble, to play with all our hearts, to enhance each other's gifts, and to embrace our diversity. God delights when we play our song in unity with passion and purpose.

At Boot Camp, John Eldredge made the point that each one of us needs a band of like-minded brothers around us, or we will never survive the war. He also said we need men who know us well and who will serve with us in a mission bigger than ourselves. I knew he was right and that I badly needed some close Christian warriors in my life. The Enemy had worked overtime to keep me isolated, and his tactics were successful for many years. This time, however, when I returned from Boot Camp, I was determined to gather a group of brothers in the Lord. I bought the *Wild at Heart: A Band of Brothers* DVD and started asking the Lord who to invite to join this circle. Several names came to mind, so I started inviting men to join me on this journey.

I barely knew one guy the Lord put on my heart to invite, and I felt a little awkward approaching him. One morning before church, though, I said, "God, if You put Rich in my path, I will invite him." I got to church early to set up for worship, and the next thing I knew Rich was right in front of me striking up a conversation. I explained "the band" to him and asked if he would be interested. He immediately said, "Yes." Three others had already accepted my invitation, so about a month after Boot Camp, my band of brothers met for the first time. At first we were all a little tentative, but after a couple of weeks God began to unify us. We went from barely talking the first night to, by the fourth week, having in-depth conversations about our struggles and fervently praying for each other. It was a watershed experience that all of us desperately needed in our lives.

Through my friendships with these men, God has shown me how vital and powerful unity is in spiritual warfare. God created us for fellowship and blesses it: "where two or three are gathered together in

My name, I am there in the midst of them" (Matthew 18:20). When my band gets together, God is in our midst, and we all feel it. The Spirit not only shows up at our meetings, but overflows into our personal lives. We all have better family and church relationships because of our commitment to meet, pray, and fellowship together. This group has been life-changing and faith-changing. In addition to our regular meetings, we've gone rappelling, rock climbing, backpacking, and skeet shooting together. I would never have experienced any of these if I hadn't stepped out of my comfort zone and extended the invitations.

So I implore you: if you don't have a close fellowship of men in your life, start praying for that now—and pray fervently. You need brothers beside you because you are in the trenches; a united front with fellow warriors is imperative for survival in this war. It also makes life a lot more enjoyable to share the journey with some intimate allies.

THE POWER OF ONE

There is one body and one Spirit, just as you were called in one hope of your calling; one Lord, one faith, one baptism; one God and Father of all, who is above all, and in you all.
EPHESIANS 4:4–6

We Christians are one in Christ, and this oneness is essential if the church is to accomplish its mission. Paul said "one" seven times in these two verses, emphasizing that we are in this fight together and that unity is essential to maintaining victory. Our Enemy's mission is to divide us and conquer us, but the Lord has let us know that if we stand as one body, with Him as the Head, we are unconquerable. We are one in Christ: we know His strength as well as the strength of numbers and the power of a unified church.

And although we Christians find so many things to disagree about, we should all be able to agree on Paul's seven points of oneness we just read in Ephesians 4:4–6. Together, we are the body of Christ, and we walk in the power of one Spirit. Our one hope is for our one Lord to return on that great day. We all share in one faith and are baptized into one body. Finally, our one God and Father has adopted us into His family and now lives inside each of us. We have so much common ground on which to take our stand together.

Besides, allowing the Enemy to divide us over church doctrine makes us look foolish to the world we are supposed to be witnessing to. How is it, they wonder, that we serve the same King, but can't sit in the same room together?

God's warriors should both pray for and promote unity in the body. We should be peacemakers who understand the struggle is not against flesh and blood, but against the forces of evil working behind the scenes to divide us (see Ephesians 6:12). Satan understands and fears the power of a unified church. He knows that warriors linking arms and walking in their authority in Christ will be his undoing.

Unity is a natural law God Himself ordained, and it actually applies to believers and unbelievers. Consider, for example, that although their hearts were not right, Noah's descendants unified and accomplished an incredible feat when they built the Tower of Babel. God acknowledged the power of unity in His commentary on their efforts: "The people are united... nothing they set out to do will be impossible for them" (Genesis 11:6 NLT). Likewise, nothing is impossible for us who follow Jesus if we stand united with Him against the forces of evil.

BODY BUILDING

To each one of us grace was given according to the measure of Christ's gift. Therefore He says: "When He ascended on high, He led captivity captive, and gave gifts to men"... for the equipping of the saints for the work of ministry, for the edifying of the body of Christ.
EPHESIANS 4:7–8, 12

I have an old Christmas picture on my dresser from when I was about four years old. In it, I am proudly wearing a blue and black Batman mask that Santa left under the tree. As a kid, I loved Batman, and that mask had to be one the greatest gifts I ever received as a little tyke. My mom tells the story of a high-spirited kid who would tie a white towel around his neck, put on the Bat-mask, and—in nothing but his skivvies—leap over and off tall furniture in a single bound (oops, that's Superman). My mission was to strike down all evil villains who dared enter our home. When I put on that mask, I was transformed into the greatest superhero on the planet. I was empowered by the gift.

God loves superheroes as well. He's created trillions of them. They look a lot like you or the guy next door. He has created every hero with special world-changing gifts and abilities. Unfortunately, there is a kryptonite, spread by the Enemy, called unbelief, and it can easily disable our power. One drop of it is like getting a buzz job from Delilah: we become weak and powerless (see Judges 16:17–20).

So, after heralding the power of a unified church, Paul listed the gifts Christ gives to those who will lead the charge to equip His church: apostles, prophets, evangelists, pastors, and teachers. The people in such leadership positions should be using these gifts to instruct and equip God's people for "the work of ministry." That call to ministry is universal. We all have a part to play, and God empowers us to play our parts well.

In all His infinite wisdom, God assembles us in groups of people who, working together, have unlimited potential to do great things for the kingdom. My friend Darrell always says, "You can go into any church, anywhere, and all the gifts of God are there whether people are utilizing them or not." That is both encouraging and sad. Every church on the planet has all of the gifts available within its congregation, but too many of those churches may never even tap into the incredible resources God has provided.

In the verses above Paul taught that God gave gifts "to each one of us." If you feel you have no gift to offer or your contribution isn't important, you've been hit with kryptonite. By grace, God gives each of us a gift or sometimes a combination of gifts, so we can build up His body, the church. He didn't exclude or miss anyone, and He knows exactly how our particular gifts can impact the church as well as the world around us.

A discussion of each gift could be a whole book in itself, but I will list them here and reiterate that discovering and utilizing our gifts is imperative for our warrior mission. If we are not exercising our gifts or don't know what they are, the body of Christ suffers. Once we discover our gifts, we either develop them, or they lie dormant. If the latter happens, the people we are supposed to be influencing aren't getting what God intended.

We can see the incredible work of the Trinity in the passages listing the gifts. There are gifts of the Father, gifts of the Holy Spirit, and gifts of the Son of God. Just a side note. In the New Testament, after each listing of the Spirit's gifts, Paul's next topic is the imperative to love each other. Without love, the gifts are empty.

Gifts of the Father (Romans 12:6–8) *Prophesying, teaching, serving, encouraging, giving, leading, and showing mercy.* These are life-purpose or motivational gifts and the Holy Spirit enhances them as we use them to serve God. We each possess a mix of some or possibly all of the gifts listed, but we usually have one or two dominant gifts used to serve the body. Not sure what yours are? Pray about it. Ask Jesus to show you. It will probably be something you already love to do and that comes naturally to you. Beyond that, you can find spiritual gift assessment tools online or ask for guidance at your church.

Gifts of the Holy Spirit (1 Corinthians 12:4–11) *The word of wisdom, the word of knowledge, faith, healing, the working of miracles, prophecy, discerning of spirits, different kinds of tongues, and the interpretation of tongues.* These are manifestation gifts that reveal the Holy Spirit's supernatural power that is available to every believer. The Holy Spirit distributes these gifts to strengthen the body of the church. Our duty is to be open and available to the Spirit at all times so that we can be a vessel He can empower in any of the nine ways listed above.

Gifts of the Son (Ephesians 4:11) *Apostles, prophets, evangelists, pastors/teachers*

> His gifts were [varied; He Himself appointed and gave men to us] some to be apostles (special messengers), some prophets (inspired preachers and expounders), some evangelists (preachers of the Gospel, traveling missionaries), some pastors (shepherds of His flock) and teachers. (Ephesians 4:11 AMP)

The gifts of the Son are given for leadership in the church. These people are empowered to make sure that spiritual gifts are understood and being used effectively in the body. Gifted to do so, these leaders should be teaching, training, and equipping warriors for the battle...

> till we all come to the unity of the faith and of the knowledge of the Son of God, to a perfect man, to the measure of the stature of the fullness of Christ. (Ephesians 4:13)

Several years ago I did a forty-day fast to pray for some breakthroughs in my life. On the last day of my fast, a friend invited me to a prophecy class down on Music Row in Nashville. I was a little skeptical, but decided to check it out. I ended up talking with a woman that night who said she had a word from the Lord for me. She said that God was about to use me in a mighty way in my workplace and that "the fields were ripe and white for harvest." This woman had no idea what I did for a living or anything about me, for that matter. I went home that night and didn't think any more about it.

The next day at work we were having a big kick-off meeting for the new fiscal year. We had a great afternoon with good food and fellowship, and as I closed the meeting, I told my employees I wanted to say a prayer and put our new year in God's hands. I spoke for a few minutes about what Christ had done to transform my life and then began to pray. As I was praying, I felt the Holy Spirit telling me to give an invitation. *What? Seriously?* Although we distributed Christian Bibles and books, this was a place of business with a diverse group of employees from many nations and religions. I tried to dismiss it, but the Spirit wouldn't let up. Toward the end of my prayer I said, "Uh, since we are talking about new starts today, I feel led to ask if anyone here needs a new start and would like to give their life to Christ. If so, please raise your hand so I can pray for you." Nervously, I looked out at the fifty or so employees in front of me—and five hands were up. Five! I prayed for them to receive Christ right there in the middle of that dusty old warehouse!

I didn't connect the prayer to the prophecy until later that day, but when it finally dawned on me what had transpired, I was, well, awestruck! God opened up a whole new world to me that day. The fields were truly ripe, five souls were harvested into the kingdom, and the Spirit had told me beforehand—through a woman I had never met—that this was going to happen! I learned firsthand that the gifts of the Spirit are real.

For the church to be whole, healthy, and advancing in power, we need to be using our gifts. After all, superheroes need their superpowers. So we need to ask ourselves, "Do I know what my gifts are? Am I using them to build up those around me? Do I really believe all of this, or has exposure to kryptonite taken me out?"

Peter said it well:

> God has given each of you a gift from his great variety of spiritual gifts. Use them well to serve one another. (1 Peter 4:10 NLT)

THE LIFE OF GOD

You should no longer walk as the rest of the Gentiles walk, in the futility of their mind, having their understanding darkened, being alienated from the life of God, because of the ignorance that is in them, because of the blindness of their heart; who, being past feeling, have given themselves over to lewdness, to work all uncleanness with

greediness. But you have not so learned Christ, if indeed you have
heard Him and have been taught by Him, as the truth is in Jesus.
EPHESIANS 4:17-21 (EMPHASIS ADDED)

We human beings are born into sin. We are the walking dead with no
hope for a future life apart from accepting Christ. Just look at some
of the words Paul used to describe those who don't know the truth:
darkened, alienated, ignorant, blind, lewd, unclean, and *greedy.* But right
in the middle of this depressing narrative, Paul pointed to another
way—"The life of God." The word *life* in Greek is *zoe,* and it means the
exuberant, eternal life in Christ that begins the moment we accept Him.
Zoe is "the state of one who is possessed with vitality; absolute fullness
of life; a life active and vigorous, devoted to God."[5] The bottom line is, if
we are not walking in this fullness, we are letting ourselves be robbed of
the life God promises us. The Bible tells us that Jesus *is zoe:*

In Him was life [*zoe*], and the life was the light of men. (John 1:4)

"I have come that they may have life [*zoe*], and that they may
have it more abundantly." (John 10:10)

"I am the way, the truth, and the life [*zoe*]. No one comes to
the Father except through me." (John 14:6)

We have the life of God within us and coursing through us: Jesus, the
Lion of Judah, abides in our hearts. Still, to know and walk in the life of
God, the old must die daily. Only then can we embrace the new.

OUT WITH OLD, IN WITH THE NEW

Put off, concerning your former conduct, the old man which grows
corrupt according to the deceitful lusts, and be renewed in the

*spirit of your mind, and that you put on the new man which was
created according to God, in true righteousness and holiness.*
EPHESIANS 4:22–24

One morning, a few weeks after I gave my life to Christ, I was reading
the Word, and the Spirit of God was illuminating it and filling my
soul. I remember announcing excitedly to Cindy, "I think I am filled
with the Holy Spirit—and I don't even know what that means!" The
presence of the Spirit within us is key to the advance. You can sit and
read the Word all day long and it not change you, but when the Holy
Spirit illuminates it, transformation happens.

One verse in particular became my refuge in those early days of
my faith: "If anyone is in Christ, he is a new creation, old things have
passed away; behold all things have become new" (2 Corinthians
5:17). It was the best news I had ever heard. I wrote the verse on a
sticky note and tacked it on my PC at work. It served as a constant
and glorious reminder that I was not the same man I used to be. My
old, sinful nature had vanished; a new man had been born. It was not
something I'd had to accomplish; it was done for me. I just had to
believe and then receive the gift by faith. The work of Christ on the
cross had set me free to be the new creation God had designed me
to be.

The "old man" is our former life in Adam—in sin—that leads only
to condemnation. The "new man" is who we are after being reborn in
Christ and experiencing *justification*: our holy God treats us "just as
if we'd never sinned." The verses above call us to action, though: "put
off" the old and "put on" the new. We must turn away from the old
man and his ways, then put on the new man who was created to be
like Christ.

The new man walks in Christ's righteousness and holiness.
Completely forgiven and washed clean, the new man is being rebuilt,
day by day, into a warrior servant prepared to take on the powers

of evil and undaunted by the task. The new man fully trusts his Commander to both restore him and empower him for his mission. Granted, it's a work in progress that continues into the next life, but that transformation starts now:

> Being confident of this very thing, that He who has begun a good work in you will complete it until the day of Jesus Christ. (Philippians 1:6)

God created us, in His own image, to be world changers because that's what He is. And we can be world changers because God's plan is to—by His Spirit—continually renovate and renew us: "'Not by might nor by power, but by My Spirit,'" says the LORD of Hosts" (Zechariah 4:6). It's God's Spirit who does the work in me. He is my power, strength, wisdom, gifting, and hope. It is this new life within me that changes things around me.

One of the Bible's greatest examples of transformation into a new man has to be Paul, originally called Saul. Just look at the dramatic change that happened in him. First, the before:

> Now Saul was consenting to [Stephen's] death.... He made havoc of the church, entering every house, and dragging off men and women, committing them to prison...
>
> Then Saul, still breathing threats and murder against the disciples of the Lord, went to the high priest and asked letters from him to the synagogues of Damascus, so that if he found any who were of the Way, whether men or women, he might bring them bound to Jerusalem. (Acts 8:1, 3; 9:1–2)

But on his way to Damascus, Paul had an encounter with Jesus that dramatically changed his story. He was instantaneously transformed into the new man. It wasn't long before he was preaching in the synagogues that Jesus is the Son of God.

Then all who heard were amazed, and said, "Is this not he who destroyed those who called on this name in Jerusalem, and has come here for that purpose, so that he might bring them bound to the chief priests?"

But Saul increased all the more in strength, and confounded the Jews who dwelt in Damascus, proving that this Jesus is the Christ. (Acts 9:21–22)

Saul had gone from Christian hunter…to hunted Christian:

Now after many days were past, the Jews plotted to kill [Saul]. But their plot became known to Saul. And they watched the gates day and night, to kill him. Then the disciples took him by night and let him down through the wall in a large basket.…

So [Saul] was with [the apostles] at Jerusalem, coming in and going out. And he spoke boldly in the name of the Lord Jesus and disputed against the Hellenists, but they attempted to kill him. (Acts 9:23–25, 28–29)

Having put off the old man and put on the new man, Paul was filled with the Holy Spirit and now boldly proclaiming the gospel he had fought so hard to snuff out. A once zealous Pharisee was now a valiant warrior preventing and undoing the works of the devil just as his King before him had done. Paul was now a soldier in the Lord's army, and the Enemy knew him by name (see Acts 19:15).

Does the Enemy know your name? If not, he will soon enough.

DARE TO BE DIFFERENT

Putting away lying, "Let each one of you speak truth with his neighbor," for we are members of one another. "Be angry, and do not sin": do not let the sun go down on your wrath, nor give place to the devil. Let him who stole steal no longer,

but rather let him labor, working with his hands what is good,
that he may have something to give him who has need. Let
no corrupt word proceed out of your mouth, but what is good
for necessary edification, that it may impart grace to the
hearers. And do not grieve the Holy Spirit of God, by whom
you were sealed for the day of redemption. Let all bitterness,
wrath, anger, clamor, and evil speaking be put away from you,
with all malice. And be kind to one another, tenderhearted,
forgiving one another, even as God in Christ forgave you.

EPHESIANS 4:25–31

Paul started out Ephesians 4 with the seven "ones" of unity, and he ended the chapter with seven areas of conduct that characterize the new man. We'll call this our "Warrior Code of Ethics." If we are to be effective in the kingdom, all of our relationships must be in good order. We should therefore examine our lives often, diligently guard our conduct, and be willing to die to self as we love and serve those around us. So below is the contrast—new man vs. old man—as well as the armor of God I saw within these exhortations. This boxing match will indeed be a fight to the finish. In this corner…

Honesty vs. Lying (v. 25) – *Put on the belt of truth!* David said, "Behold, You desire truth in the inward parts" (Psalm 51:6). Walking in the Spirit guides us into all truth (see John 16:13). When the truth is deep inside us, honesty is the hallmark of all our relationships.

Righteous vs. Unrighteous anger (v. 26) – *Put on the breastplate of righteousness!* It is not a sin to get angry. Christ Himself got angry, but His was a righteous anger and He didn't hold on to it. The book of Psalms tells us twice that God is "slow to anger" (103:8, 145:8). The book of Proverbs tells us three times that *we* should be slow to anger (15:18, 16:32, 19:11). If we are slow to anger, we will not allow that anger to take over, and pausing before we speak is a key strategy. Satan will try to trap us, but we must let go of anger and not hold grudges.

Guarding our lives vs. Giving Satan a foothold (vv. 26 – 27) – We stand our ground in *the shoes of peace*, guarding our lives and pressing forward with our *shield of faith* raised. Many times, with our actions or our words, we give the devil permission to wreak havoc in our lives. Always looking for an entrance point into our hearts and our lives, Satan watches what we say and do so he can ensnare us. We don't want to empower evil or give the Enemy an open door, so we must guard ourselves against the temptations of the world and the flesh. Also, when we don't resolve a conflict and we go to bed angry, we are sinning. We need to try to reconcile before the sun goes down, or we leave ourselves vulnerable to Enemy attack.

Generosity vs. Stealing (v. 28) – Be hardworking and generous. As Christ's warriors we should be an example of integrity, honesty, and generosity in our workplaces as well as our homes. We should also be unselfish with our time and treasure. If there is a need we can meet, we should be quick to meet it.

Edifying vs. Corrupt speech (v. 29) – *Take up your sword and speak the Word!* The Enemy gives us many opportunities to fall into his trap of gossip, slander, and crude language. David said in Psalm 141, "Set a guard, O LORD, over my mouth; keep watch over the door of my lips" (v. 3). Those wise words are good to pray. When we do speak, Paul said, we should be encouragers and impart grace. Edifying speech should be the norm for us. People should be coming to us because they feel better about themselves when they leave our presence.

The book of Proverbs gives us great words of wisdom about our speech:

- The mouth of the righteous is a well of life. (10:11)
- The tongue of the wise promotes health. (12:18)
- A man has joy by the answer of his mouth. (15:23)
- Death and life are in the power of the tongue. (18:21)

The Bible has much to say to us about the power of our words. We should diligently guard our mouths and choose to speak encouraging words that build people up.

Obeying vs. Grieving the Holy Spirit (v. 30): We need to be sensitive to the Spirit's leading. He will warn us before we plunge into sin—but we have to be listening. When we do sin, we need to be quick to repent, to break any agreements we've made with the Enemy, and to be reconciled to God.

Positive vs. Negative behavior (v. 31): *Guard your mind by putting on the helmet of salvation and renewing your mind in the Word!* Bitterness, wrath, anger, clamor, evil speaking, and malice are all devices the Enemy will use to get a foothold in our lives. That's the old man. Replace those traits with kindness, tenderheartedness, and forgiveness. "Overcome evil with good" (Romans 12:21). Also, Jesus said that offenses will come (see Luke 17:1), so we need to learn to be ready and willing to forgive. When I think of all the grace and forgiveness God has extended to me, I find it truly astounding. Equally astounding is how easily I can justify holding a grudge against people. God is simply asking me to extend to others the grace He has lavished on me.

> **Battle Strategy:** Know and choose to live out these traits in your daily walk: be truthful, temperate, on guard, hardworking, generous, an encourager, sensitive to the Spirit, kind, and forgiving. Don't give the Enemy a foothold in your life.

THE TAKEAWAY

As a warrior in Christ, I declare that ...

- I will follow His lead and "walk worthy of [my] calling" (Ephesians 4:1).
- I will be humble, gentle, patient, and—in love—allow for others' faults (4:2).
- I will promote unity of the Spirit and peace with those in my circle of influence (4:3).
- I will use my gifts to equip, empower, and encourage others (4:7–12).
- I will rely on the Spirit to help me live according to Christ's standards (4:13).
- I will speak the truth in love today (4:15).
- I have put off my old nature (4:22).
- I will renew my mind daily in the Word of God (4:23).
- I am a new man created by God in true righteousness and holiness (4:24).
- I will be completely honest in everything I say today (4:25).
- I will not let anger dominate the day, nor will I go to bed angry with anyone (4:26).
- I will not give the devil a foothold in my life (4:27).
- I will work hard and with complete integrity (4:28).
- I will give generously out of what God gives me, trusting that He will continue to meet my needs (4:28).

- I will not say any corrupt or evil words but instead use my speech to build people up (4:29).
- I will walk in holiness and not hinder the work of the Spirit in me today (4:30).
- I will rid myself of all bitterness, rage, anger, slander, and evil behavior today (4:31).
- I will be kind and tenderhearted; I will forgive everyone as God, in Christ, forgave me (4:32).

Father, I ask You to empower me to walk boldly in Your Spirit as I follow You. Help me to promote unity in the body. Strengthen me to walk worthy of my calling as Your son and a warrior in Your army. I pray for closer connections with Your people. Help me also to establish and maintain a close brotherhood of men to fight the battle with. Reveal to me the gifts You have blessed me with and help me use them so I am a blessing to those around me. I put off all my former conduct as the old man and put on the Lord Jesus Christ to walk as the new man today. I commit to stand strong in the Warrior Code of Ethics and dare to be different so people will see that difference and know that I live for You. May my life bring You glory. In Jesus' name I pray. Amen.

WAR ROOM DISCUSSION

1. *If it seems way out of your comfort zone, there's a good chance it is God's calling.* When have you found that to be true in your life? Be specific.

2. Why would the unity of Jesus' followers be essential to accomplishing the mission of the church, to sharing the gospel with the watching world?

3. What are your spiritual gifts? In what ways are you using those gifts for the Lord's work—or in what way would you like to be using them?

4. Discuss what it means to let your old self die, to "put off… the old man… and… put on the new man" (Ephesians 4: 22, 24). Brainstorm practical ways you can both *put off* and *put on*.

5. Which of the seven points of the Warrior Code of Ethics do you find most challenging? What will you do to more consistently choose the behavior that pleases the Lord? Who will you ask to pray for you and hold you accountable?

READ EPHESIANS 5

7

COURAGEOUS
WALKING IN THE SPIRIT

If we live in the Spirit, let us also walk in the Spirit.
GALATIANS 5:25

*If you're not pursuing a dangerous quest with your life,
well, then, you don't need a Guide.*
JOHN ELDREDGE[1]

Be imitators of God as dear children.
EPHESIANS 5:1

"I would follow him to hell and back. So would the men of E company."
That is a quote from a World War II veteran from Easy Company
about his commander. Major Dick Winters was such a courageous
servant leader that the men of the 506 Parachute Infantry Regiment
would and did follow him anywhere—even into the fiercest, most
dangerous battles of the war like the Brecourt Manor Assault,
Operation Market Garden, and the Battle of the Bulge, to name a
few. These men had a fearless leader and a noble cause worth fighting
for, worth dying for. I submit to you that our cause, our war, is even
more noble and our leader, both incomparable and unconquerable.
Our war also requires soldiers of great faith and courage who are
willing to, figuratively speaking, follow their leader to hell and back
if necessary.

In Ephesians 5, Paul spoke to the new men who are walking in the Spirit. He exhorted us to walk in love, light, and wisdom; to be good husbands, fathers, employers, and employees; and to set an example by being Christlike in all our relationships. This kind of God-honoring lifestyle, my friend, will take tremendous courage. It will take a mighty warrior.

In this chapter Paul's first directive for us was to "be imitators of God." Really? How exactly do we do that? We can look to the Son for insight, for Jesus said, "Anyone who has seen me has seen the Father" (John 14:9 NIV). C. S. Lewis said, "The Son is the self-expression of the Father—what the Father had to say; and there never was a time when He wasn't saying it." Referring to Christ, 1 John 2:6 says we should "walk just as He walked." Have you studied Jesus' walk lately? He was so close to His Father that He said, "I and My Father are one" (John 10:30). Hebrews 1:3 (NIV) states, "The Son is the radiance of God's glory and the exact representation of his being!"

So to imitate God, we'll need to closely examine the life of His Son so we can follow in His footsteps and imitate Him. Jesus said that if we want to be His followers, we must do three things: deny ourselves, take up our cross daily, and follow Him (see Luke 9:23). To be a true disciple of Christ, we put aside our self-centered ways and walk through each day with a servant's heart and in our Lord's footsteps.

Check out Paul's intense commitment to follow Christ:

> I consider my life worth nothing to me; my only aim is to finish the race and complete the task the Lord Jesus has given me—the task of testifying to the good news of God's grace. (Acts 20:24 NIV)

Forsaking all, Paul was determined to fulfill God's call on his life at any cost. He walked the path courageously in the power of the Holy Spirit. In fact, Paul endured all he went through and still maintained his unshakeable faith because he relied on the Holy Spirit's empowerment.

Paul wasn't superhuman; his secret was being surrendered completely to Christ. Paul's allegiance was to his Commander King, and he really didn't care if he lived or died serving Him. Paul laid down all of himself and all of his life for Christ and for those God called him to serve.

Jesus was also wholeheartedly committed to the Father's plan: "Did you not know that I must be about My Father's business?" (Luke 2:49). So Jesus walked the road of suffering—and He walked it willingly. Jesus knew exactly what His God-given mission on this earth was. He knew He would shed His blood in order to blaze the warrior path for all of us.

Jesus was, without question, the most courageous and compassionate warrior to ever set foot on the planet. He was fierce yet kind; strong yet meek; bold yet humble; unafraid of confrontation yet loving and merciful. And Jesus called His disciples to walk with the same boldness, courage, and compassion that He did. But here's the good news: just as the Holy Spirit descended on Jesus before He began His ministry (see Matthew 3:16–17), Jesus sends us the Spirit to guide and empower us in our ministry. The power of the Holy Spirit within is the key to our walking in courage.

I am reminded of a great line from the movie *Robin Hood* where this leader of his band of Merry Men says, "Rise and rise again, until lambs become lions!" I love that. No matter how many times the Enemy knocks us down, we can—in the power of the Spirit—rise again stronger than before! God will use our adversity to strengthen us and enable us to overcome our Adversary. God will make sure we become valiant, heroic warriors as we stay the course. And why wouldn't we stay the course? After all, He created us to be men of courage!

THE GREATEST... IS LOVE

Walk in love, as Christ has loved us and given Himself for us,
an offering and a sacrifice to God for a sweet-smelling aroma.
EPHESIANS 5:2

Though we are entrenched in spiritual war, our war with the Enemy is not to be the focal point of our lives. We are to focus on God, and God is love. Because of His immense love for us, God sent His Son as a sacrifice: His death atoned for our sin so we could be reconciled to the Father. God is holy, so reconciliation with sinful man could only be accomplished through a blood sacrifice: "without the shedding of blood there is no forgiveness" (Hebrews 9:22). Jesus said during His ministry, "There is no greater love than to lay down one's life for his friends" (John 15:13), and He willingly laid down His life for you and me. So loving others and laying down our lives for them is one way we imitate Christ. A good soldier in God's army walks in love by putting others' needs ahead of his own. Maybe you should make that phone call you've been putting off. Maybe you should strike up a conversation with that person you've been avoiding. Ask the Lord, "How do You want me to make a difference in someone's life today?"

One day I was talking with Darrell about not sharing my faith as often as I should. He looked at me and said matter-of-factly, "You don't really love people then." *Excuse me?* It took a minute to choke down my pride enough to admit that he had nailed it. I wasn't willing to step out of my comfort zone for the people around me whom I knew were perishing. My prayer life began to change that day. I started asking God to humble me and help me to love people the way He does, to help me make the most of every opportunity He gives me to share the gospel—the Good News—of Jesus' love.

The really incredible thing about walking in love is we don't have to try and conjure it up ourselves. We can't give away what we don't possess, but—as we saw in chapter 5—the Spirit fills our hearts with love (Romans 5:5) as we walk in step with Him. We can then, in turn, love people the way God intends and the same way He loves us: unconditionally. So we ask our Father to fill our empty cups daily with what He has in abundance—and that is love. He pours the Mighty River of His Spirit into our hearts, and we become conduits of our King's love: He loves and ministers to others through us. As I've mentioned, we're not fighting *for* victory, but *from* victory. Similarly, I heard someone say once, "We're not working *for* the love of God; we're working *from* the love of God."

If you want to know how you are doing in your love-walk, you need look no further than Paul's magnum opus on love in 1 Corinthians 13. Here we see the selfless love of Christ that is the hallmark of the Spirit-filled life:

> Love is patient, love is kind. It does not envy, it does not boast, it is not proud. It does not dishonor others, it is not self-seeking, it is not easily angered, it keeps no record of wrongs. Love does not delight in evil but rejoices with the truth. It always protects, always trusts, always hopes, always perseveres. Love never fails. (1 Corinthians 13:4–8 NIV)

Now I would ask you to read those verses once again, but this time replace the words *love* and *it* with *Christ*. Now read it another time but insert your own name. That 1 Corinthians 13 description of love is the standard. That is the benchmark for walking in love. How are you doing?

WALK IN THE LIGHT

Let there be no sexual immorality, impurity, or greed among you. Such sins have no place among God's people. Obscene stories, foolish talk, and coarse jokes—these are not for you. Instead, let there be thankfulness to God. You can be sure that no immoral, impure, or greedy person will inherit the Kingdom of Christ and of God. For a greedy person is an idolater, worshiping the things of this world. Don't be fooled by those who try to excuse these sins, for the anger of God will fall on all who disobey him. Don't participate in the things these people do. For you were once full of darkness, but now you have light from the Lord. So live as people of light.

EPHESIANS 5:3–8 NLT

Two kingdoms fight in this spiritual war: the kingdom of light and the kingdom of darkness—and they are not equal.

Before giving my life to Christ, I woke up countless days having no recollection of what I had done the night before. My goal each night was to annihilate the demons that had harassed me all day long. I needed to medicate my misery, and I did so by drinking myself into a state of blissful unawareness, also known as a blackout. I didn't realize I was not only increasing the darkness, but actually partnering with it as well. The lies I believed about myself had led to a life of excess and addiction. Those were dark days, and the Enemy had me right where he wanted me. Even when I walked around in the full light of day, I was shrouded in darkness. By the time I was twenty-five, I had been arrested three times for drunk driving, I had totaled two cars (which meant a short stint in jail), and I had adversely impacted countless lives with my self-centered habits. It's only by God's grace and mercy that I didn't kill myself or, even worse, an innocent bystander.

The day I accepted Christ into my heart, He began to illuminate my life. I had met the Light of the world. And although the darkness has tried desperately to cling to me, the light of Christ continually overwhelms it:

> In Him was life, and the life was the light of men. And the light shines in the darkness, and the darkness did not comprehend it. (John 1:4–5)

By the Spirit, the life of Christ as well as the truth of His Word flood our hearts with light. But the light isn't meant to be contained within us. The purpose of light is to overtake darkness, and we are to share that light. Even the smallest beam of light pierces the pitch-black void of a dark room and brings a degree of illumination. Similarly, we who are being filled with the Spirit of Christ shine His light into this dark world. Jesus said, "As long as I am in the world, I am the light of the world" (John 9:5). Since Jesus is no longer physically on this earth, what is the source of light and truth and hope?

"You are the light of the world. A city that is set on a hill cannot
be hidden.... Let your light so shine before men, that they
may see your good works and glorify your Father in heaven."
(Matthew 5:14, 16)

God intends for us, His people, to be beacons of light wherever He has
placed us. He knows that people are watching to see if we are authentic,
to see if our light is real or artificial. The Enemy also watches us. He is
ready to move in and get a foothold should we misstep. Satan's job is
obvious: snuff out the light in us before it can chase away the darkness.

The other day a friend of mine observed, "Many times we empower
evil." He went on to say that he examines his life all the time because
he doesn't want to give Satan any access. Those are wise words, and we
should heed them carefully. When we knowingly sin, we empower the
Enemy... and our light fades.

Are we maintaining our integrity when we watch television or surf the
Internet? Are we guarding our mouths and choosing words wisely? Do
we stand on our principles when people challenge our godly behavior,
or do we compromise our faith in order to look good in the world's eyes?
Are we greedy for gain, or do we regularly express thanks to God for all
that He's given us? Such are the choices that set us apart from the world.
We are called to "cast off the works of darkness, and ... put on the armor
of light" (Romans 13:12) if we are to be beacons in this dark world.

So how do we increase the light? "The entrance of Your words gives
light" (Psalm119:130). To walk in more light, we need to sunbathe in
the Word daily. We need to soak it up. God will illuminate His written
Word and fill our hearts with His light. Then our light will penetrate
this dark and dying world wherever we go.

You are a chosen generation, a royal priesthood, a holy nation,
His own special people, that you may proclaim the praises of
Him who called you out of darkness into His marvelous light.
(1 Peter 2:9)

WALK IN WISDOM

Walk circumspectly, not as fools but as wise, redeeming the time, because the days are evil. Therefore, do not be unwise but understand what the will of the Lord is.
EPHESIANS 5:15-17

We need wisdom. Actually, we need God's wisdom. Without it, we truly don't stand a chance in the battles we face. In Old Testament times, being wise "was viewed as a mastery of the art of living according to God's expectations."[2] The ancients believed that wisdom developed over time through the study of God's truth and life experiences with Him. The result was "the knowledge and ability to make the right choices at the opportune time."[3] In other words, their wisdom increased over time as they walked with God each and every day. Thousands of years later, the answer is the same for us: we walk with God, and He imparts wisdom for the way.

One incredible definition I found for the word *wisdom* is "skill in war."[4] And God's wisdom absolutely brings skill in spiritual warfare! Taking it a step further is one of my favorite "wisdom" verses: "Wisdom is the principal thing; therefore get wisdom" (Proverbs 4:7). So that verse could be written: "Skill in war is the principal thing; therefore get skilled in war." Am I reaching? Maybe, but I don't think so. God intends for us to be skilled warriors and to walk in victory by walking in His wisdom.

Wisdom is also defined as "shrewdness" which, in turn, means "dangerous" and "marked by clever discerning awareness."[4] I don't know about you, but I like the sound of those definitions. It would definitely be a great thing if my spiritual enemies considered me a dangerous spiritual warrior with clever discerning awareness.

Maybe most important, Proverbs reveals the prerequisite for receiving God's wisdom: "The fear of the LORD is the foundation of wisdom" (9:10 NLT). A humble, reverent respect for and a genuine awe at God's greatness and majesty will enable us to receive the wisdom and knowledge we desperately need on our journey.

Last, Jesus Himself is the embodiment of all wisdom: "You are in Christ Jesus, who became for us wisdom from God" (1 Corinthians 1:30). Jesus *is* wisdom. And since we abide in Him and He in us, all spiritual wisdom is available to us. So study Christ. Hear His counsel—and act on it. Read the Word. We can only walk in wisdom if we know Scripture and apply its truth to our lives.

As I mentioned in chapter 3, Paul prayed for the Ephesians to receive the Spirit of wisdom and revelation. The Greek word *wisdom* in the New Testament means "spiritual and practical wisdom, skilled, an expert."[5] The way to become an expert at anything is by working diligently at it day by day.

God is the Source of all wisdom and knowledge, and He gives it freely to His faithful warriors. When you need wisdom for whatever circumstances you may be facing, here is the promise: "If any of you lacks wisdom, let him ask of God, who gives to all liberally and without reproach, and it will be given to him" (James 1:5).

Battle Strategy: Faithfully study the Word and then, moment by moment throughout the day, ask Jesus to impart to you His wisdom.

FILL MY CUP

Don't drink too much wine. That cheapens your life. Drink the Spirit of God, huge draughts of him. Sing hymns instead of drinking songs! Sing songs from your heart to Christ. Sing praises over everything, any excuse for a song to God the Father in the name of our Master, Jesus Christ.

EPHESIANS 5:18–20 MSG

I hit mile marker nine with my tank almost completely on empty—and *tank* refers to my body. Running my first (and only) half marathon in 2008, I had trained for three months and was in the best shape of my life. The problem was, I had trained on a treadmill and a flat track. The course through downtown Nashville meandered up and down rolling hills, and I was fading fast. At mile marker nine my legs were cramping, and I seriously considered dropping out. But as I rounded the corner, onto Music Square East, I heard music up ahead. Belmont Church had set their praise band up outside, and they were playing "All the Earth Will Sing Your Praises," one of my favorite songs. As I praised God—and huffed and puffed—the Spirit kept me on a worship high that carried me the next 4.1 miles to the finish line—and I beat my target time!

God delights in our worship of Him. And I know that when I praise Him with my whole heart, He shows up and fills me with His fullness. The apostle Paul also experienced being filled with the Spirit, and in the passage above, he compared it to drunkenness, which is great news to anyone who overindulged in the party life like I did. There are many reasons why I drank: to feel good, to fit in, to overcome my fears. Alcohol was liquid courage for me. Paul seems to be saying that being drunk is a counterfeit to the real deal, to being filled with the Spirit! Think about it. The fruit of the Spirit is love, joy, peace… It sounds like walking in God's presence, intoxicated by the Spirit, would provide all I ever tried to find in a bottle. Jesus told us to drink in the Spirit deeply (John 7:37–38). As He fills us, we joyfully praise Him and thank Him.

Just like getting drunk requires time (and a lot of alcohol), being filled with the Spirit requires time. The more time we spend in the Lord's presence, the more fully we can expect to be filled by His Spirit and the love, joy, and peace He longs to give us. It's not a one-time-fills-you-forever experience. We are continually filled with the Spirit as we regularly read His Word, engage in worship, and give thanks to God. Sometimes I just open the book of Psalms, and as

I start reading and speaking the passionate words of the psalmists, the anointed words begin to fill me. I also keep a playlist of worship songs on my iPod and play them throughout the day to reconnect with my Lord. The other prerequisite to being more filled with the Spirit is—ask for more! Jesus said, "How much more will your heavenly Father give the Holy Spirit to those who *ask* Him" (Luke 11:13, emphasis added).

Worship also has a way of transforming any situation, good or bad, into a God encounter. Case in point. I recently went on a backpacking trip with some guys from church. It was a grueling hike as we climbed one of the highest peaks in the Smoky Mountains. I hadn't exercised before the hike the way I should have, so my strength was sapped long before we reached the top. Though physically wiped out, I made it to the peak, and we camped overnight on top of the mountain.

The next morning I woke up feeling even more exhausted. We packed our gear and started our descent when suddenly the skies opened up and let loose a torrential downpour. (This trip just kept getting better!) It rained so hard that the water got under my rain gear and soaked my clothes; the flooded path drenched my socks and shoes.

About an hour into the journey, sopping wet and totally miserable, I could hear these words coming from behind me:

> When I survey the wondrous cross
> On which the Prince of glory died,
> My richest gain I count but loss,
> And pour contempt on all my pride.

It was a fellow hiker singing one of my favorite old hymns. Those powerful words pierced my heart, so I joined in on the next verse—and the next. At one point we came to a log bridge across a raging mountain stream, and we stopped right in the middle of it and worshiped God, with our hands raised, in the pouring rain. It was awesome!

The power of worshiping our God transformed one of the worst weekends of my life into a worship experience I will never forget. The weary trek down that mountain in the middle of a downpour ended up being an epiphany: God showed me that worship is the key to turning dismal days into times of triumphant praise!

God wants to meet with us anywhere, anytime—not just at church on Sunday. He is available on muddy trails, in family crises, at the unemployment office, in the homeless shelter, in that big meeting at work—wherever His people are praising Him, He is there in the midst. He inhabits the praises of His people (see Psalm 22:3). So keep a song of praise in your heart. Speak it, sing it, shout it—and let God use it to lift you above your circumstances.

WORSHIP AND WARFARE

> When [the magistrates] had laid many stripes on [Paul and Silas], they threw them into prison, commanding the jailer to keep them securely. Having received such a charge, he put them into the inner prison and fastened their feet in the stocks.
>
> But at midnight Paul and Silas were praying and singing hymns to God, and the prisoners were listening to them. Suddenly there was a great earthquake, so that the foundations of the prison were shaken; and immediately all the doors were opened and everyone's chains were loosed.
>
> ACTS 16:23-26

I don't know about you, but if I had just been beaten, thrown in prison, and had my feet bound in stocks, I'm not sure my first order of business would be to start singing hymns even though it should be. God responded to Paul and Silas's unrelenting faith by shaking the foundations of the prison they were in and freeing everyone from their chains. Don't miss that! Prayer and praise break chains and free us from whatever is binding us. Are you under attack? Are you deep in the pit? Sing to the King! Praise from the pit brings victory from above!

Another great example of the power of worship in warfare is in 2 Chronicles 20. In that passage we also see the stand, walk, and war process when Jehoshaphat, the king of Judah, found himself on the brink of annihilation. Judah was surrounded by three powerful enemies who had joined forces and were marching straight toward them.

When Jehoshaphat learned of the multitude coming against them, he gave us a shining example of what to do to gain victory over our enemies: Jehoshaphat went into spiritual warfare mode. Up against what looked like impossible odds, Jehoshaphat declared a fast and started praising and praying to God in the midst of the assembly.

God replied, "You will not need to fight in this battle. Position yourselves, stand still and see the salvation of the Lord, who is with you. Do not fear or be dismayed; tomorrow go out against them" (v. 17). Notice that God told them to *stand* still and then to go, to *walk*. The *war* step gets really interesting. Jehoshaphat bowed down, face to the ground, and worshiped God. Then he assembled the singers and praise band and had them line up in front of the army. He instructed them to start marching toward the oncoming battalions, still singing and praising God. Think about it. Decimation was marching straight at Judah, and Jehoshaphat sent out the praise band!

In response to Judah's faith, God threw the enemy into confusion, and they started destroying each other. By the time Judah reached the battlefield, no enemy was left. Instead the armies of Jehoshaphat saw before them a sea of dead bodies. This incredible story clearly shows us the immense power of worship in spiritual warfare.

Last, I will never forget the worship at Boot Camp. There were no singers or musicians. We sang to a CD, but I had never felt such power and unity in worship. It felt like four hundred warriors going into bloody battle. Many of us were singing at the top of our lungs with our arms raised in total abandon. At one point, a fellow warrior behind me slapped his hand over my shoulder as we roared through a chorus of "Great I Am." I felt the power of God in a way I never had before. I can't really do it justice with words, but I still think about it quite often. I came out of that experience a different man. I was ready to serve my King and fight for my family. I could no longer sit on the couch and let life pass me by. I had connected with my God in a new and vital way.

On the bus ride back to Denver, I asked a new friend from camp why he thought the worship was so incredibly powerful that we experienced at Boot Camp. He said, "Desperation!" And he was right. I think we all knew this was a unique opportunity to meet with God like we hadn't in a while, and we were desperate to connect with Him—to hear His voice, feel His touch, experience His power. We needed Him to show up and help us believe we were going to be effective warriors for His kingdom—and He did. He made a grand appearance in that theater in the Rockies and left an indelible impression on me. He answered the desperate cry of my heart. Get desperate, warrior. Worship your King!

> **Battle Strategy:** Keep a song of praise in your heart and sing it often. Worship the King and watch the enemy run and flee!

HONOR YOUR VOWS

The husband provides leadership to his wife the way Christ does to his church, not by domineering but by cherishing. So just as the church submits to Christ as he exercises such leadership, wives should likewise submit to their husbands.

Husbands, go all out in your love for your wives, exactly as Christ did for the church—a love marked by giving, not getting. Christ's love makes the church whole. His words evoke her beauty. Everything he does and says is designed to bring the best out of her, dressing her in dazzling white silk, radiant with holiness. And that is how husbands ought to love their wives. They're really doing themselves a favor—since they're already "one" in marriage.

No one abuses his own body, does he? No, he feeds and pampers it. That's how Christ treats us, the church, since we are part of his body. And this is why a man leaves father and mother and cherishes his wife. No longer two, they become "one flesh." This is a huge mystery, and I don't pretend to understand it all. What is clearest to me is the way Christ treats the church. And this provides a good picture of how each husband is to treat his wife, loving himself in loving her, and how each wife is to honor her husband.

EPHESIANS 5:22-33 MSG

Am I providing strong leadership for my wife? Am I cherishing her each day? Am I speaking words that evoke her beauty and bring out the best in her just as Christ does for His church? Although I fail often, when I actually make a point of putting Paul's words into practice, I see my wife's spirit rise up. I can tell she feels more secure when I show her how much I care and that I'm fighting for her. The Enemy attacks her constantly and will stop at nothing to make her feel like her life is insignificant, that her words and ideas aren't important. All it takes is her realizing I have zoned out for a few seconds when she is talking (not that I ever do that!), and the Enemy starts screaming in her ear, "See? He doesn't give a rip about you and your opinion." I know the Evil One does the same to men, but he seems especially brutal to women.

When I go out of my way to show Cindy how important she is to me, it always makes a huge difference. Sometimes I get a glimpse of the innocent little girl as she lights up with joy. Those are princess moments, priceless moments. Next thing I know, she is doing nice things for me—texting me prayers and saying encouraging words to me. I don't do it for those reasons, but the fruit of building up my wife is, well, glorious. Furthermore, God says it's my job. That's right. He wants my wife to be whole and holy, and my prayers and encouragement make a huge difference in seeing that come to pass. I was designed to be the leader, warrior, and priest of my home, so if my marriage is less than what God desires, I am ultimately responsible.

I'm not saying it's always my fault when Cindy and I have problems, but I am supposed to be the leader. When I say something without thinking, make her feel inadequate in some way, or just don't listen when she's talking, I see her light fade and her heart shut down. The Enemy has then successfully divided and conquered my wife and me; our strength as one flesh is temporarily snuffed out. When that happens, I need to be strong enough to apologize. Also, when we've had an argument and need to reconcile, I have found it helpful to banish the spirits that are coming between us before we talk.

The bottom line is, we warriors need to walk in love and ask for God's intervention in our marriages. I read somewhere that a married man can't become all that God created him to be without the prayers and support of his wife, his "helper," as she is called in Genesis. No question. We were made to be a cohesive unit, and there is real power in our unity as man and wife when we, as one flesh, are serving our God.

Clearly, we who call ourselves "warriors" need to walk in wisdom and to pray for our marriages and our homes. Peter said it like this:

> Husbands, dwell with them with understanding, giving honor to the wife, as to the weaker vessel, and as being heirs together of the grace of life, that your prayers may not be hindered. (1 Peter 3:7)

Hindered prayer is exactly what we don't need. Hindered prayer means the Enemy can come in like a flood and wreak havoc in our lives. But if we daily honor our wives and ask God to protect our marriages, then together we will inherit the grace of life. The grace of Christ.

A good friend of mine asks God to help him stand strong on the frontlines for his family. He wants the Enemy to know he has to first go through him before he could ever get to his wife and kids. Knowing that Chris is a mighty prayer warrior, I am sure that his wife and family are secure. If you're not the prayer warrior for your family that you want to be, stop reading. Put down the book and ask God to help you become the prayer warrior and the husband your wife needs, one who will bring out the best in her.

Battle Strategy: Love, honor, and cherish your wife. Pray and ask for God to help you stand strong and courageous as the appointed leader of your home.

RAISING WARRIORS

Fathers, do not provoke your children to anger by the way you treat them. Rather, bring them up with the discipline and instruction that comes from the Lord.
EPHESIANS 6:4 NLT

It's interesting that Paul pointed the verse above directly at fathers. We are supposed to be leading our children as we follow Christ. We are to set the example and guide them:

You must commit yourselves wholeheartedly to these commands that I am giving you today. Repeat them again and again to your children. Talk about them when you are at home and when you are on the road, when you are going to bed and when you are getting up. Tie them to your hands and wear them on your forehead as reminders. Write them on the doorposts of your house and on your gates. (Deuteronomy 6:6–9 NLT)

Is the Word of God the prized possession in our homes? Do our kids know we are living by its standards and guidelines? Its principles should be evident in what we say and do. Words from Scripture should be woven throughout our conversations and highly revered in our homes. God revealed to Joshua that the secret to having a rich Christian life is to not only meditate on but also constantly speak His Word.

> This Book of the Law shall not depart from your mouth, but you shall meditate in it day and night, that you may observe to do according to all that is written in it. For then you will make your way prosperous, and then you will have good success. (Joshua 1:8)

Commitment to the Word of God is imperative for living in a way that honors God, for having a marriage that reflects the love between God and His church, for strengthening the family unit, and for raising children to know and love the Lord. I read recently that 50 percent of all American children can expect their families to break up before they reach the age of eighteen. Half of us dads don't have to worry much about provoking our kids to anger—they aren't even in the same home with us. That is disastrous!

Where are the warriors? Where are the godly men who will stay and fight for their sons, daughters, wives, and homes as commanded in Nehemiah 4:14? The Enemy is winning his war against our families, he is dominating, and we don't even recognize that he is a big contributor to the problems of divorce and broken homes, among many other problems. We keep fighting the flesh-and-blood battle with our wives, our kids, and even ourselves, but—as Paul said in Ephesians 6—our battle is actually against Satan and his evil armies who passionately desire to destroy our families and our faith in God.

So are we men fighting the wrong battle, or have we become passive like Adam, sitting idly by as the world and the Enemy plunder our families? I wonder how I will answer to God Himself for all the times I turned on the television when I should have been spending quality time with or going to war for my family. Even though Operation Steal, Kill, and Destroy is being conducted against my home, many times my response has been to pick up the remote and check out. But those days are behind me. I'm sick to death of losing. I was created to be a victor. God is for me, and if God is for me, who can be against me? He has given me everything I need to win the battle for my home.

I believe winning this war for our marriages and homes starts with men—specifically, men who rely on God and trust Him completely. We have to respond to the critical need. We have to man up. And I am really not preaching to you as much as I am exhorting myself and letting you listen. I have been passive most of my life, but I didn't understand the battle the way I do now. I no longer have an excuse to do nothing.

We men were made to come through, fight back, and persevere under trial. God commands us to take courage. Many days I don't feel courageous, but I heard someone say recently, "Courage is like a muscle: the more often you act courageous, the more courageous you become." The Word of God and the power of the Holy Spirit combine to make us strong and courageous as we step out of our comfort zones and do the things God calls us to do to protect our families.

It seems right to close this chapter with a promise and exhortation God gave Joshua. The Lord's promise to Joshua is His promise to all of us:

"No one will be able to stand against you as long as you live. For I will be with you as I was with Moses. I will not fail you or abandon you. Be strong and courageous." (Joshua 1:5 NLT)

THE TAKEAWAY

As a warrior in Christ, I declare that...

- I will follow Christ and be an imitator of God (Ephesians 5:1).
- I will walk in love because Jesus has loved me and gave His life for me (5:2).
- I will not take part in sexual sin, covetousness, foolish talk, or coarse joking (5:4).
- I will give God thanks in everything and walk through life with a grateful heart (5:4).
- I will walk as a child of light and have no fellowship with the works of darkness (5:8–14).
- I will walk in God's wisdom today, redeeming the time He gives me (5:15–16).
- I will both surrender to and be filled with the Spirit of God today (5:18).
- I will worship God in the Spirit with psalms, hymns, and spiritual songs (5:19).
- I will love the church as Christ does (5:22–33).
- I will love, cherish, and fight for my wife every day (5:22–33).
- I will leave a godly legacy by encouraging my children to love and obey God (6:4).
- I will serve Christ in my daily work and be obedient to my employer (6:5).
- I will walk courageously in the power of the Holy Spirit today.

WAR ROOM DISCUSSION

1. What are some reasons why living a life that honors God takes courage?

2. Why is our knowledge and study of God's Word essential to the light we shine in this dark world?

3. Think of a time when, after you acted on the promise of James 1:5, God provided you with the wisdom you needed either through His Word or one of His people.

4. When has worship—figuratively speaking—helped you finish a half marathon? Or what current half marathon might be eased if you choose to worship God in that situation?

5. If you are married, in what specific ways are you loving your wife the way Christ loved His church? In what ways are you her spiritual leader and protector?

6. What are you doing to protect your family? In what situation does God need you to exercise your courage muscle on behalf of your family? What will that look like?

Heavenly Father, I ask You to conform me more and more into the image of Christ today as I live to imitate Him. I pray that, by Your Spirit, I will walk in more power, love, light, and wisdom than ever before. Fill me with all the fullness of Your love, so I can pour it out to those I encounter today. Give me ears to hear Your voice as I walk the path in the light of Your presence. Remind me to live with a mind-set of worship and stay close to You today, filled with Your abundant life. I surrender my home, my marriage, my family, and myself to You. Lead me and teach me to be a better husband and father. Show me creative ways to bless and cherish my wife, and I thank You for making us heirs together of the grace of life. In Jesus' powerful name I pray. Amen.

READ EPHESIANS 6

8

EQUIPPED
READY FOR MY MISSION

THE ARMOR

*Spiritual Christians look upon the world not
as a playground but as a battleground.*

A. W. TOZER[1]

When I was a few months into writing this book, my band of brothers
and I decided to have our first Advance study. We prayed for guidance,
and then each of us invited some men to join us for the eight evening
sessions. The morning of the first session, Cindy and I had a falling out
over some weekend events and went our separate ways in anger. The
Enemy had caught us in his trap even before we'd finished our morning
coffee! Satan's Operation Divide and Conquer was underway.

Later that morning I called Darrell to see how he was doing and to
pray with him about the evening. He told me that his foreman of eight
years had just quit without giving any notice. This was more than a big
setback for his business. Darrell had considered the man a good friend,
and they had parted ways on a bad note. The war was on!

By noon I finally had at least a degree of peace. Then the phone
rang: my dad—who lived in another state—was unconscious and being
rushed to the hospital. It turned out, his blood sugar had dropped to
an unbelievable low of 14. Recognizing the spiritual warfare as well as

the significant threat to his life, I texted my band of brothers, and we all started praying. By 2:00 p.m., my dad was awake and having lunch, but by this point I was more than a little rattled.

Then, as we were getting underway that evening, everything that could possibly go wrong—did. First of all, one by one, the guys we invited got stuck in Darrell's long, winding driveway. He had recently paved it, and the weekend's torrential rain had softened the asphalt to where you couldn't get a car up to his house. After forty-five intense minutes, we finally got everyone into the house. We were ready to begin... only to find that our DVD player and computer equipment weren't working. Of course all the technology had worked perfectly when we had tested it earlier in the day. The Enemy was pulling out all the stops.

Finally—and despite all the attacks—we got everything working and had a great first night. As the night progressed, all the men became engaged in the material and awakened to the battle God had called them to fight. After we wrapped up, I was exhausted—but encouraged. I don't recall ever going through so many battles in a single day, but God walked me through each one, moment by moment, step by step.

The following night I got a phone call at 2:00 a.m. A deer had run out in front of my daughter's car as she was driving home from work. She swerved and hit an electrical box, totaling her car. Thankfully, she wasn't hurt, but she only had liability insurance on the car. The accident meant the loss of her only means of transportation, and she didn't have money for a new car.

Later the following day, my wife called me at work. She was in tears. She had simply stood up after tying her shoes, and for no apparent reason her back went out. She had never had any back problems, but she could barely walk for four days. All coincidence? I hardly think so. Our Enemy is determined, and He will do anything to block our attempts to expose him and advance the Gospel. By the time the weekend rolled around, I was battle weary.

The Enemy had waged an all-out war that week, and I had underestimated his power. I took some shots for sure, as did Darrell, my dad, my daughter, and my wife—but I didn't feel defeated. I clearly knew, though, that it was time to re-examine the battlefield, that I needed more training for the battles, and that my King would teach me how to be effective in this war.

WAGING WAR

By wise counsel you will wage your own war,
and in a multitude of counselors there is safety.
PROVERBS 24:6

Until recently, I didn't really understand this verse: what did the Bible mean by "wage your own war" and have "a multitude of counselors"?

One day I asked the Lord where I would find *my* "multitude of counselors," and in that very moment, I looked over at a bookshelf packed with Bibles and Christian books (thankfully, Cindy loves to collect books). Right then—by God's grace—I realized, *I don't have to know my counselors personally.* There, right in front of me, I had a multitude of amazing counselors at my disposal 24/7. So, for the first time in my life, I began reading all I could about spiritual warfare, and God began showing me in His Word and through these counselors how I could fight the good fight.

To succeed in this war, you will have to read too. If it's not your favorite pastime, ask God to give you a love for reading—especially for reading His Word. (Since God gave us His truths in written form, He has to have put some affection for reading in all of us.) Start small and build up your reading time as you go. Also, get the Bible and books on warfare in audio form. Many days I spend my drive time listening to my counselors, so I can strengthen my battle skills each day.

In addition to reading God's Word as well as other resources He has provided, we need to develop the habit of asking for wisdom and revelation as we walk through our day. Even the Son of God was not self-reliant when He walked the earth: He said Himself, "I can of Myself do nothing" (John 5:30). "Filled with the Holy Spirit" (Luke 4:1), Jesus submitted Himself to the Father's will, obeyed His Word, and waged His war under the direction of the Holy Spirit. Acts 10:38 says, "God anointed Jesus of Nazareth with the Holy Spirit and with power, who went about doing good and healing all who were oppressed by the devil, for God was with Him" (Acts 10:38).

The war Jesus fought and that we, His followers, fight today is spiritual and invisible, but the Spirit of God *will* reveal to us the battle strategy we need. Our becoming a skilled warrior begins when we acknowledge our desperate need for the Holy Spirit's guidance and counsel. We must seek first His wisdom and revelation to know how to fight, and then we must rely on His strength when we enter the battle we would surely lose without Him.

We wage our own war by knowing and trusting God's promises; by walking in the power of the Spirit; by putting on the full armor every day; and by learning how to use our weapons of spiritual warfare effectively.

WHERE DOES MY HELP COME FROM?

Be strong in the Lord and in the power of His might.
EPHESIANS 6:10

One morning when I was in the middle of writing this book, I awoke from a fitful night of dreaming about warfare, and I had a word from the Lord on my mind. It was just one word—but it's a word that every warrior must understand and come to terms with. Are you ready for it?

The word—the reality—is *weakness.*

I sensed that God wanted me to acknowledge just how weak I am in my flesh. I focused on that humbling reality for most of the day, and then God revealed part two of His assignment for me: meditate on His power. That's what Ephesians 6:10 is telling us. Apart from God's power, Satan and his legions of darkness will be our undoing. They are incredibly powerful, much too strong for us in our mortal flesh. Even the most muscle-bound, Arnold Schwarzenegger-looking dude on the planet is no match for Satan's evil forces without the power of the Spirit. For this reason Paul exhorted us to "be strong in the Lord and in the power of His might." In our own strength, we don't stand a chance.

David understood this principle. He proclaimed, "It is God who arms me with strength" (Psalm 18:32). David knew he had to rely on God to win his many battles against his formidable enemies. As we prepare to fight the Enemy, we must submit to God. Then, once we're on the battlefield, we must rely solely on His strength, power, wisdom, and revelation. Again I quote Zechariah: "Not by might, nor by power but by My Spirit, declares the Lord" (4:6). Only by recognizing our own weakness and trusting in God's infinite power can we walk through the battlefield of life in victory. I might be able to achieve in my own strength some of the things the world considers great, but accomplishments of eternal significance can only be done if we are completely surrendered to God's power and will.

The more I thought about this divine arrangement, the more freeing I found it. All my insecurities, weaknesses, and failures—none of those matter. None of those will keep me from succeeding because God's power is all I need. Both you and I can do all things through Christ who strengthens us (Philippians 4:13). Just as the apostle Paul did—and countless saints through the millennia have done—you and I can trust God and rely on Him for strength. And it's especially easy to receive that strength when we feel we have none of our own.

Think about it. Moses didn't part the Red Sea: God did. Gideon didn't cause the whole Midianite army to flee using water pots and trumpets: God did. David didn't slay a giant and his ten thousands in his own strength: the Spirit worked through him. Even Jesus' many miracles were not done in His own strength—He was filled with the Spirit of God!

As I already mentioned, Paul heard the definitive word on weakness from Jesus Himself: "My grace is sufficient for you, for My strength is made perfect in weakness." Paul continued: "Therefore most gladly I will rather boast in my infirmities, that the power of Christ may rest on me ... For when I am weak, then I am strong" (2 Corinthians 12:9–10).

Weakness acknowledged invites power: God's power. And His power is all we need to overcome the Enemy.

> **Battle Strategy:** Acknowledge your weaknesses to God. Then spend time reading about and meditating on His mighty power (Psalm 18, Psalm 147:3–5, 2 Corinthians 13:4, Hebrews 1:3).

AXIS OF EVIL

Put on the whole armor of God, that you may be able to stand against the wiles of the devil. For we do not wrestle against flesh and blood, but against principalities and powers, against the rulers of the darkness of this age, against spiritual hosts of wickedness in the heavenly places.
EPHESIANS 6:11–12

In my freshman year of high school and without really any forethought, I joined the wrestling team. I vividly remember my first match. My opponent was about my size, but he looked like he had been wrestling since birth! He was well built and equipped with all the fancy gear. I got down on all fours in the bottom/down position, and he stood in the advantage/top position above me. Within seconds of when the referee called out, "Wrestle," I was on my back and close to being pinned. I had quickly discovered that my opponent was well trained, agile, and strong. I remember exerting every ounce of energy I had to avoid being pinned, but it was futile. I was out-skilled and overpowered. Within a minute or so, the match was over. I remember feeling defeated and demoralized. I just wanted to quit—and that is exactly what our Enemy is hoping for in this spiritual wrestling match we find ourselves.

This wrestling is up-close and personal. Our Enemy will use all his skill and maneuvering to try to pin us down and make us think we have no hope of escaping our situation. But let's remember: we fight from victory! We just need to sharpen our skills. When Satan seems to have us pinned, we need to know a reversal move that will quickly get us back on top and having the advantage. The word *wrestle* means "to engage in or as if in a violent or determined struggle; to combat an opposing tendency or force."[2] We are in the wrestling match of our lives, so we must be skilled in the ways and weapons of warfare which we will look at more in chapter 10.

Ephesians 6:10–12 confirms that spiritual war is upon us whether we like it or not. Paul told us plainly that the battle is not against people ("flesh and blood," v. 5), but against the invisible forces of evil. Now I'm not going to give Satan more attention than he deserves, but Paul said our battle is not against people. Our Enemy is causing a lot of the conflict we face, so we must learn to recognize and defend ourselves against the real source of the attacks we experience.

We also learn from these Ephesians 6 verses that the Devil is a master strategist who commands a celestial hierarchy of evil. Paul mentioned four divisions in Satan's army, and they appear to be listed in order by rank, going from most powerful to least:

- Principalities (*arche*): "chief, first, magistrate, power, rule."[3] These appear to be archangels; the most powerful angels in the order of Michael. They are probably territorial spirits that control entire nations (see Daniel 10:13).
- Powers (*exousia*): "force, potentate, delegated influence, magistrate, one whose will and commands must be obeyed by others."[4] A *magistrate* is a local official, so this rank may rule over smaller areas such as states or cities.
- Rulers (*kosmokrator*): "a world ruler: epithet (subordinate) of Satan: spirit powers."[5] This Greek word *kosmokrator* sounds

like something right out of a sci-fi movie! Their name indicates they have a high position and authority to rule.

- Spiritual forces of wickedness (*poneria*) - "depravity, iniquity, a vicious disposition."[6] I believe these are Satan's vile minions, his foot soldiers. They are probably the ones we are contending with on a regular basis.

Satan truly is the commander of an enormous, organized, and powerful evil army. I don't know how Paul could have made it any clearer. We believers are not at war with each other; our battle is with satanic forces working behind the limited reality we see and experience.

Paul revealed deep mysteries here. How did he know these wicked battalions exist and their specific ranks? For one thing, he had been to the third heaven (2 Corinthians 12:2), and, as he said in Ephesians 3, the Spirit had revealed great mysteries to him. Paul had been given incredible insight about the spiritual realm.

Much like the Nazis' hated and vowed to annihilate the Jews in World War II, these evil spiritual forces hate God and all of His offspring. Their goal is to secure their prisoners (the lost), hinder or destroy God's people, and stop the advance of God's kingdom on earth. And just as the Nazis were under Hitler's command, these fallen angel armies pledge their complete allegiance to Satan and his cause.

If you are still skeptical about the strength and strategy of our Enemy, don't take my word for it. Consider what Jesus and the apostles said about the Wicked One and his mission. He has declared war against all of God's people:

> The dragon was enraged with the woman [the church], and he went to make war with the rest of her offspring [Christians], who keep the commandments of God and have the testimony of Jesus Christ. — John in Revelation 12:17

"The thief does not come except to steal, and to kill, and to destroy." — Jesus in John 10:10

Stay alert! Watch out for your great enemy, the devil. He prowls around like a roaring lion, looking for someone to devour. Stand firm against him, and be strong in your faith. — Peter in 1 Peter 5:8–9 NLT

The world around us is under the control of the evil one. — John in 1 John 5:19 NLT

"Satan, the ruler of this world, will be cast out." — Jesus in John 12:31 NLT

You once walked… according to the prince of the power of the air. — Paul in Ephesians 2:2

These are some eye-opening verses—from reliable sources—about the Enemy of our souls. He has declared war on us, and the Lord expects us to fight. Time to suit up!

FULL ARMOR

Take up the whole armor of God, that you may be able to withstand in the evil day, and having done all, to stand.
EPHESIANS 6:13

Imprisoned and perhaps chained to a Roman guard while awaiting trial, Paul referred to the pieces of that soldier's armor when he described the spiritual battle gear we need in the invisible war. Every piece of the armor was vital to the soldier's survival on the battlefield, and the same is true for the armor God gives His warriors who are fighting a spiritual battle.

We are embarking on a dangerous path through Enemy territory, so we must always be prepared for attack. Walking in the armor must be our way of life. God has provided it for our protection on our journey. In fact, Paul described putting on the armor as putting on Christ Himself:

> Let us cast off the works of darkness, and let us put on the armor of light.... Put on the Lord Jesus Christ. (Romans 13:12, 14)

Christ is the armor. He is our truth, our righteousness, our peace, our faith, and our salvation. He is also the Word (our sword) that became flesh. We are to put on the shining armor of Christ and no longer entangle ourselves in the evil works of darkness. In fact, we are commanded to pierce the world's darkness with the light of Christ and to tell the gospel news of Jesus' love and forgiveness throughout the earth.

Think back for a moment over everything Paul laid out in Ephesians 1–5. What a rock-solid foundation we have! In addition to that foundation, God has given us amazing—and divine—armor so we can fight fearlessly against the Enemy. Our armor shouldn't stay pristine for long, however. When we reach heaven, it should be well worn from many battles in the trenches. I heard Christian comedian Brad Stine speak at a men's conference, and I loved his take on the armor:

> I believe by faith that one day when I enter into that new place, I will stand before Jesus Christ, and He alone will remove my armor. And when I stand in that place, I want my shoes rotted on the bottom. I want my shield dented to heck. I want my breastplate beat up. I want my sword bloody and broken in half and my helmet falling off, because when I go down, I want to go down a warrior! So then God can release me and say, "Go forth, son! You've done well, and the fight's over. Let's go home!"

THE BELT

Stand firm then, with the belt of truth buckled around your waist.
EPHESIANS 6:14 NIV

The belt of truth is the first piece of armor we put on, and it guards us against the Enemy's lies and deception. If we are not 100 percent certain of who we are, what we stand for, and who stands with us, we will not fare well in the heat of battle. Standing on God's truth is foundational, and we build on it day by day as we read the Bible and apply its truth to our lives. The Word is the ultimate God-confidence builder. David said it this way: "His faithful promises are your armor and protection" (Psalm 91:4 NLT). The time we spend reading, studying, and memorizing Scripture today prepares us for the battles we will encounter on the path ahead.

The Bible declares that God cannot lie, and that means everything in God's Word is absolute truth. Jesus said the truth liberates us: "You shall know the truth, and the truth shall make you free" (John 8:32). Knowing the whole truth as revealed in God's Word brings true freedom, but consider that Jesus made this statement: "I am the way, the truth, and the life" (John 14:6). So we need to know the truth as God presents it in the Bible, and that kind of knowing we do in our head. We also need to know the Truth as Jesus lived it out, and that kind of knowing is more a matter of the heart. Intimately knowing Jesus—God's living Word—and the Bible—God's written Word—is an essential element of our armor.

Likewise, a Roman soldier's belt was vital to his prowess in war: he clipped his shield to it and hung his sword and dagger on it. This belt was the Roman equivalent of the duty belt that police officers wear today. Among the tools police officers have on their belts are a firearm, extra clips for that firearm, a flashlight, a night stick, a taser, handcuffs, and pepper spray. Not knowing what they may face each day, they have to be armed and ready for anything.

And this analogy reveals just how crucial the belt of truth is for the spiritual warrior. Being a student of the Bible and knowing the truth it proclaims protects us from believing the incessant lies of the Enemy. As I've pointed out, Jesus said that Satan "is the father of lies" and "there is no truth in him" (John 8:44 NIV). Satan masterfully twists God's words to make the misquote sound like the truth. "You will not surely die," he proclaimed to Eve (Genesis 3:4). He is using the same tactics today that he used in the Garden. He works hard to get us to doubt God's promises and faithfulness. Walking with the belt of truth on, however, gives us spiritual discernment and enables us to know when the Enemy is speaking his native language of lies and deception. We need that discernment "lest Satan should take advantage of us; for we are not ignorant of his devices" (2 Corinthians 2:11).

The belt also beckons us to walk in strong character and integrity. Are we living a life of truth, or have we been deceived, allowed to think we can get away with certain sins? The belt calls us to be honest with ourselves and with God. Now, God already knows about all of our sins and struggles, so if we've given in to temptation, why not just confess it and repent? Follow David's example as he prayed, "You [God] desire truth in the inward parts... Wash me, and I will be whiter than snow" (Psalm 51:6–7).

Just as the Roman soldiers and today's police officers do, we need to have our duty belts and the right spiritual tools on them: repentance, humility, wisdom, honesty, morality, and integrity are vital. We are to wear the truth, so buckle up, warrior, and walk in the truth and with the Truth, with Jesus Himself.

THE BREASTPLATE

Put on the breastplate of righteousness.
EPHESIANS 6:14

The breastplate of righteousness guards our hearts from the Enemy's condemnation. A Roman soldier used his breastplate to guard his heart and other vital organs. Clearly, the soldier's breastplate was essential in battle. He would never go into battle without it—and neither should we.

Solomon said in Proverbs 4:23, "Above all else, guard your heart." Those are wise words to heed because our Enemy is always hurling accusations and firing his slanderous darts at us. His mission is to make us feel condemned and defeated, thereby rendering us ineffective soldiers. To counter all that, God imparted His righteousness to us through Christ. Righteousness means that, in Christ, we have right standing with God and are now in a forgiven condition that is acceptable to Him. Christ's blood paid the price for all of our sin, so we are righteous before God the Father: "I no longer count on my own righteousness through obeying the law; rather, I become righteous through faith in Christ" (Philippians 3:9 NLT).

We receive God's free gift of righteousness "through faith in Christ." Simply put, it means we have been made right with God by our faith in Jesus. Once we receive this gift, we are free from all accusation. Christ did all the work necessary for us to stand—holy and blameless—before God. Whatever we've done in the past doesn't matter. We now stand righteous in God's sight because of our faith in Christ: we stand behind the breastplate of righteousness that completely deflects the condemning lies Satan hurls at us. As the apostle Paul put it, "There is therefore now no condemnation to those who are in Christ Jesus" (Romans 8:1).

Finally, it is worth noting that the Roman soldier used leather strips to attach his breastplate to his belt so the breastplate was securely in place. That fact about Roman armor tells us that our righteousness in Christ is connected to our acceptance of the truth (belt) that He is who He says He is and we are who He says we are. We must believe and stand firm on what God says about us, and He says that we are now righteous soldiers in His army.

So let's put on the breastplate of righteousness and securely connect it to our belt. We are now much better prepared for battle. The Enemy can accuse and condemn us all day long, but our breastplate guards our hearts by faith, and the stronger our faith, the thicker our body armor becomes.

THE SHOES

...having shod your feet with the preparation of the gospel of peace.
EPHESIANS 6:15

After exhorting us to stand with the belt and the breastplate, Paul addressed the shoes we need to have on our feet. So it's time to talk about moving, the second phase of the stand, walk, and war process.

A Roman soldier's sandals had spikes going through the soles that gave him great stability and traction no matter what the battle conditions. He could stand his ground firmly in bad weather, on hills, or in rough terrain, and these spikes gave him a great advantage over his enemy in hand-to-hand combat. Similarly, when we are securely grounded in God's truth and believe that we are righteous before Him, we are standing on a firm foundation and cannot be easily moved by our Enemy. We are ready to march forward confidently in Christ, boldly proclaiming the gospel of peace as God has commanded us to do.

In chapter 6, I told you about walking down the mountain in the pouring rain. At many points on the descent, the path was narrow and the ledge dropped off thousands of feet. We stopped at one point to rest, and as I stood there, my foot suddenly slid out from under me on the wet rock. I could feel the weight of my backpack pulling me backward over the cliff, and I truly thought I would momentarily be seeing Jesus in all His glory. It all happened in a split second, but it's a moment I still remember vividly. If I hadn't gotten my balance back quickly, I would indeed be hiking in heaven right now—and everyone in my crew knew it. It was a close call.

And it was very significant. You see, during the entire hike the Lord had been speaking to me about preparedness, and at that moment I realized I was not prepared for the rain and slippery mud. I didn't have the right shoes for the occasion. And that's what Paul was talking about here. Preparedness makes way for peace. It's all about readiness to proclaim the good news as we stand strong against the opposition. The more prepared we are, the more confidently we can stand and advance. And the root of that preparation and confidence is—again—spending time reading, studying, and memorizing God's Word and staying in close communication with the Commander. We prepare for spiritual battle with the Bible and prayer. There are no shortcuts.

So lace up your shoes and get ready to walk, warrior. It's almost time to go to war!

THE SHIELD

Above all, taking the shield of faith, with which you will be able to quench all the fiery darts of the wicked one.
EPHESIANS 6:16

In a scene from *Gladiator,* the Roman army fills the sky with a barrage of flaming arrows launched at their enemies. This same scene plays out in the spiritual realm 24/7, and many of those arrows have your name etched on them. You are the King's son, so you are a threat and therefore a target. These deadly accurate arrows never stop flying—and they are pointed straight at your heart.

So we pick up our shield of faith *after* putting on our shoes because "we walk by faith" (2 Corinthians 5:7). Our mission is to advance, fully trusting in God's promises and the armor He provides. Faith gives us courage to move forward despite the incoming barrage of fiery arrows being shot at us. Faith is "conviction of the truth: trust (or confidence) whether in God or in Christ: reliance upon Christ for salvation; constancy in such profession."[7] Hebrews 11:1 gives us the biblical definition: "Now Faith is the confidence of what we hope for and assurance about what we do not see." (NIV). We can be completely confident about what God says. We can speak aloud God's truth when circumstances are difficult. We can believe His promises and cling to them when life's storms rage. God's promises and His faithfulness to them are our inexhaustible hope for the battles ahead. The Bible clearly says we will have trials and testing, but we can live with joy and hope as—in Christ's strength—we battle the forces against us. We can walk in power and authority with our shields raised in faith.

In one of my favorite passages in the Bible, Jesus said what may be the greatest words ever spoken on what the power of faith can accomplish:

> "Have faith in God. For assuredly, I say to you, whoever says to this mountain, 'Be removed and be cast into the sea,' and does not doubt in his heart, but believes that those things he says will be done, he will have whatever he says. Therefore I say to you, whatever things you ask for when you pray, believe that you receive them, and you will have them." (Mark 11:22–24)

Faith is the fuel that keeps us moving forward and the incredible power that can move mountains. Simply put, faith is truth in action. We must therefore know the truth, and that's why the belt of truth is the first piece of armor we put on. Faith will work only when it is God's truth we are putting our faith in: God's truth must be the object of our faith.

So what is the mountain standing in your way? Is it fear, doubt, anger, lust, family matters, or financial problems? Jesus said to start—in faith—speaking God's truth to those mountains, and they will crumble and fall. Find the promises that apply to your situation. Then believe them, speak them aloud, and trust God to work for your good and His glory. And, at the same time, deflect the Enemy's lies head-on and with your shield of faith raised.

The Roman soldier's counterpart to our shield of faith was made of heavily woven wicker, and before he went into battle, he dipped it in water to keep it from catching on fire when incoming flaming arrows struck it. The Greek word for *flaming* (verse 16) is *puroo*, the source of our word *pyro*. Among the definitions of *puroo* is "to be inflamed (with anger, grief, lust)."[8] Satan's arrows are on fire with sin, deceit, lies, and temptation. He and his evil archers continuously launch these arrows at us in hopes that we grow weary and drop our shield, even for an instant. Clearly, we must fight this battle in God's strength and by faith in Him. Our strong faith in God shields us from the barrage of Satan's fiery arrows.

The Enemy believes he'll find a chink in our armor, but let's be sure that he finds instead an unyielding faith that stops his arrows. Having been dipped in the Living Water, our shield snuffs out the sinful flames, and our shield becomes more and more impenetrable as our faith in God increases. Paul said, "Faith comes by hearing, and hearing by the word of God" (Romans 10:17). We have clearly seen the interconnection between having faith in God, knowing the truth of His Word, and choosing to believe.

Also, we find even more strength and protection for the battle when we are experiencing unity in our churches and walking with a band of brothers. Consider this visual from pastor and writer Chip Ingram's *The Invisible War*:

[The Roman shield] had hooks on the sides to link to other shields in a line so that an entire row of soldiers could advance without exposing themselves to incoming arrows.[9]

When they linked shields, the Roman army became a formidable advancing wall that could not be easily penetrated by inbound arrows. That's what God is calling His church to be: a formidable advancing wall of warriors committed to fighting for God's people and against the Enemy.

One day, after I described this passage for my band of brothers, my pastor texted us a picture of a Roman battalion marching, some holding their shields in front of them and other soldiers holding their shields over their heads. The shields were so large you could only see the soldiers' feet. He texted two words under the picture: "Shields up."

God did not create us human beings to walk alone, much less to battle the Enemy alone. We need as much spiritual protection around us as possible.

And we need to keep strengthening our faith in our Commander because the thicker and wetter our shield becomes, the fewer Enemy arrows can penetrate it. Shields up!

THE HELMET

Take the helmet of salvation.
EPHESIANS 6:17

I have a tendency to let my mind wander, and that is rarely a good thing. I can be having a perfectly fine day, and then my mind drifts off for a moment, and suddenly I'm spiraling down the black hole of my past or dwelling on a subtle lie from the Enemy. The helmet of salvation is there to protect us against Enemy infiltrations such as these.

Salvation, in this instance, means defense and deliverance. Paul wasn't talking only about being saved because the people he was addressing his letter to—the church in Ephesus—were already believers. Here Paul's use of *salvation* was referring to us being wholly confident in our defender and deliverer Jesus, the hope of our salvation, and to always remember in the heat of battle who we are in Him—God's sons and soldiers.

Just as the Roman soldier's helmet offered protection for his head, the helmet of salvation guards our minds, which is the site of the fiercest spiritual battles. Satan's strategy is to bombard our minds with lies and deception. His goal is to give us a spiritual concussion—so to speak—in hopes we will forget who we are and how great a deliverance we have received in Christ. Satan continually spews out his propaganda and lies in an effort to distract us from the truth and to control our thought patterns. In Romans 12:2 Paul told us how to stand strong against those efforts: "Do not be conformed to this world, but be transformed by the renewing of your mind." The word *transform* is related to the word *metamorphosis*, which means "a change of physical form, structure, or substance especially by supernatural means."[10] The word *renewing* means "renovation; complete change for the better."[11]

So we who want to be strong in battle continually ask the Holy Spirit to transform our minds through prayer, and we meditate on God's Word day and night to remind ourselves who we are and how great our God is. Also essential to winning the war of the mind is fixing our mind on God's way of thinking. Paul gave us this instruction:

> Whatever things are true, whatever things are noble, whatever things are just, whatever things are pure, whatever things are lovely, whatever things are of good report, if there is any virtue and if there is anything praiseworthy—meditate on these things.... and the God of peace will be with you. (Philippians 4:8–9)

As we renew our minds and guard our thoughts, we are enabled to better hear, moment by moment, the voice of our Commander guiding us. Knowing Jesus' voice also enables us to readily identify the Enemy's voice and reject the rebellious, impure, untrue, and destructive thoughts with which he tries to fill our minds. Effective soldiers "take captive every thought to make it obedient to Christ" (2 Corinthians 10:5 NIV). If we know the thought is not from Jesus, we are to capture it and reject it.

Now, indulge me here, but we could compare the helmet of salvation to the helmet NASCAR drivers wear when they race. In it, they have a two-way radio so they can be in constant communication with their spotter. NASCAR drivers don't have wing mirrors on their cars, so they have large blind spots. The spotter is in a position to see the whole race and relay information to his driver about any cars in his blind spots or any adverse track conditions ahead. Communication with the spotter is vital so the driver knows what's going on around him at all times.

In the same way, the helmet of salvation allows us to hear the voice of our Commander who, like the spotter, sees the whole race and warns us of imminent danger on the path. Again, we are in an invisible war, so everything is in our blind spot unless we have the Spirit to guide us. He leads us through our battles as we engage in prayer, which is our spiritual two-way radio. We put on our helmet, ask for guidance, and listen for our Commander's still, small voice. The quieter and more attentive we are, especially in the midst of battle, the more clearly we hear His voice. The Word we have hidden in our hearts becomes a powerful weapon as we allow the Spirit to bring it to our minds in our battles. But more about that in a minute.

Someday we will stand before King Jesus, and He Himself will remove our helmets and replace them with a crown. That glorious day is coming soon. For now, let's be ready in our armor and listening for our marching orders. We are almost ready to get in the fight.

THE SWORD

Take... the sword of the Spirit, which is the word of God.
EPHESIANS 6:17

One year, my amazing wife bought me the perfect birthday gift: a full-sized sword. The day she gave it to me, I noticed right away that it wasn't sharpened. As I was holding it, the Lord spoke to me about the significance of the dull blade: "If your sword isn't sharp, you will be ineffective in the battle." God didn't say it in a condemning way, but the truth hit me hard: I had been neglecting the very thing that would make me razor-sharp against the Enemy—and that is God's all-powerful Word.

> The word [*logos*] of God is living and powerful, and sharper than any two-edged sword, piercing even to the division of soul and spirit, and of joints and marrow, and is a discerner of the thoughts and intents of the heart. (Hebrews 4:12)

To fully understand how the Sword of the Spirit works, we need to examine three Greek words for *word*. The three Greek words are *graphe*, *logos*, and *rhema*. *Graphe* refers to the written word: the Bible sitting on your table is the *graphe*. In Hebrews 4:12, *word* is the translation of *logos*, and *logos* is the understanding of the written Word's message. In Scripture, *logos* is the Holy Spirit revealing what the living and active Word of God means and breathing it into life inside of us. You can sit and read the Word (*graphe*) all day long and not be changed by it, but when the Spirit brings it to life, it becomes *logos*—and transforms you.

According to Hebrews 4:12, the *logos* divides our soul from our spirit man. This is significant because our soul—our mind, will, and emotions—rarely lines up with our spirit. The Holy Spirit indwells our spirit, but our souls draw us away from the holy life God intends for us. So, like a master surgeon with a razor-sharp scalpel, the *logos*—as we meditate on it and hide it in our heart—exposes and cuts away any and all hindrances, so we can receive and understand the Word, walk freely in the Spirit, and know how to pray effectively.

The *logos* also discerns the "thoughts and intents of our hearts." It penetrates our hearts and exposes the lies we believe and the wrong motives we sometimes have. *Logos* reveals our wrong thinking and replaces it with truth. This is why we need to meditate on God's Word day and night. The *logos* is like a healing balm or a nuclear bomb depending on our need. It heals and restores, it destroys Enemy strongholds, and it equips us for the battle.

"FROM HIS MOUTH CAME A SHARP SWORD"

In Ephesians 6:17 *word* is the third Greek word—*rhema*. It is the weapon of the Holy Spirit: "Take the sword of the Spirit, which is the word [*rhema*] of God." *Rhema* is "an utterance or command."[12] It is the *logos* coming out of our mouths like a sharp sword. Don't breeze by this. In warfare, having all the Bible knowledge in the world will do you no good if you don't speak its words aloud. Satan can't read your mind, and he could care less how much Scripture you've memorized unless you are piercing him with it as you speak Scripture out loud.

The *logos* cuts into the spirit realm as—with the Holy Spirit's guidance—it comes out of our mouths. We continually hide God's Word in our hearts, so when the battle rages, we have ammo at the ready. That is spiritual warfare; that is wielding the sword. We need to commit passages to memory, so keep a running list of your favorite verses in your pocket or on your smartphone and review them often. You are going to need them.

The sword Paul referred to here is actually the gladius, the smaller sword or dagger that the Roman soldier carried. It had a curved end and was razor-sharp on both sides to do maximum damage when wielded in close combat. A dull sword in the heat of close range battle is suicide, and the same is true in the spiritual realm. This piece of armor again establishes both how close our Enemy actually is and our need to be equipped to take him out quickly. If we confidently speak Scripture out loud to Satan in Jesus' name, then the father of lies—the great deceiver—will retreat.

God's Word—the Bible—is alive and powerful, giving us everything we need for spiritual victory over the Enemy. That's why true warriors keep their sword sharp and ready at all times. Joel exhorted us, "Beat your plowshares into swords" (Joel 3:10). Get the Word into your heart. Meditate on it, memorize it, hammer it out, and sharpen this sword; by God's design it is your main go-to weapon.

As I mentioned earlier, God told Joshua: "This Book of the Law shall not depart from your mouth, but you shall meditate in it day and night … Then you will make your way prosperous, and then you will have good success" (Joshua 1:8). Notice God says that His truth "shall not depart from your *mouth*." Again, we have to speak the Word of God for it to be an effective weapon in battle. When the Enemy strikes, we are to counter his attacks with the Word of God just as Jesus did in the wilderness (Matthew 4:1–11). Three times Satan attacked—and three times Jesus countered with the Word (*rhema*).

Finally, when Jesus returns at the end of history, the Word will conquer His foes: "From his mouth came a sharp sword to strike down the nations" (Revelation 19:15 NLT). That verse isn't referring to a literal sword, but to Jesus speaking the powerful Word of God and destroying all of His enemies. Likewise, we must have a sharp sword ready to come out of our mouths and fight the Enemy in the spiritual realm. The Spirit will give us the words to speak to secure our victory:

> When the enemy comes in like a flood, the Spirit of the LORD will lift up a standard against him. (Isaiah 59:19)

So how sharp is your sword? I'm guessing yours—like mine—could stand a bit of honing. What works for me is to put verses on sticky notes and tack them on my mirror to memorize when I shave. You could put additional sticky notes in your car and on your computer at work. Keep reminders all around you lest you forget you are at war—and that you are a warrior!

Putting on the armor is a mind-set, not something we just check off our list. As we prayerfully put on each piece of the armor daily, we remember that we stand on God's truth and His declaration of who we are in Christ (belt). We have right standing with God and are free from all condemnation (breastplate). We walk in Christ's peace (shoes). Our great faith in Christ protects us against the Enemy's temptations, deception, and lies (shield), our minds are confident and secure in our salvation (helmet), and we war with prayer using the Word of God (sword) against the forces of evil. When we put on this spiritual armor, we can withstand anything hell unleashes against us.

Battle Strategy: Put on the full armor daily and, as you do so, think about the specific protection each piece provides. Then take up your sword, speak the Word of God in battle, and watch the Enemy flee.

176 THE WARRIOR'S ADVANCE

THE TAKEAWAY

I declare that, as a warrior in Christ, I will ...

- Be strong in the Lord and rely on His power only (Ephesians 6:10).
- Put on the full armor of God today and be ready to take my stand against the forces of evil (6:11).
- Use spiritual armor to fight my spiritual enemies (6:12).
- Stand on God's promises with my full battle gear on (6:13).
- Wear the belt of truth and stand on God's Word with honesty and integrity (6:14).
- Trust that the breastplate of righteousness will guard my heart from the Enemy's condemnation (6:14).
- Walk in the shoes of peace and diligently prepare to advance the gospel (6:15).
- Take up the shield of faith that defuses the Evil One's fiery arrows (6:16).
- Put on salvation as my helmet to guard my thought life (6:17).
- Take up the sword of the Spirit and wield it against my Enemy (6:17).
- Pray in the Spirit at all times and on every occasion (6:18).
- Pray for boldness to open my mouth and make known the mystery of the gospel (6:20).

Lord, thank You for equipping me for spiritual battle with each piece of Your armor. I strap on the belt of truth and stand on Your Word that protects me from all the lies and deception of the Evil One. I put on the breastplate of righteousness that guards my heart from condemnation and shame. I stand strong in the shoes of peace that give me confidence to move forward and advance the Gospel. I take up the shield of faith that defuses all of Satan's fiery arrows. I put on the helmet of salvation and receive the mind of Christ so I can clearly hear Your voice and walk in step with You. Give me a renewed love and passion for Your Word and, in the heat of battle, may it be a sharp sword coming forth from my mouth by the guidance of the Holy Spirit. In Jesus' name I pray. Amen.

WAR ROOM DISCUSSION

1. What freedom and blessings can come when we befriend our weakness?

2. We don't want to give Satan more attention than he deserves, but at the same time we need to recognize not only his very real presence and power, but also that of his four-tier army. What can you do to keep that balanced perspective?

3. Comment first on the appearance, design, and purpose of each piece of armor worn by a Roman soldier in battle. What is one characteristic you found especially ingenious?

The Belt	The Breastplate
The Shoes	The Shield
The Helmet	The Sword

4. Now explain what each piece of armor means to you as you fight spiritual battles. Which detail of every piece listed here makes you especially confident about using it in spiritual warfare? Why?

> The Belt of Truth
> The Breastplate of Righteousness
> The Shoes of the Gospel of Peace
> The Shield of Faith
> The Helmet of Salvation
> The Sword of the Spirit

5. What do you do to put on this armor of God? How do you start your day?

9

EQUIPPED
READY FOR MY MISSION

PRAYER WARRIOR

*All Christian power springs from communion with
God and from the indwelling of divine grace.*
JAMES H. AUGHEY

*[Pray] always with all prayer and supplication
in the Spirit, being watchful to this end with all
perseverance and supplication for all the saints.*
EPHESIANS 6:18

As he neared the end of his letter to the Ephesians, Paul brought his
exhortations to a grand crescendo with this final instruction: pray
always—and always in the Spirit! After all, we have well established the
fact that the spiritual realm is directly affecting the world around us, so
we must learn to war in that realm.

Yet even as we acknowledge the importance of prayer, making it a
priority in our lives can be one of our greatest struggles. Personally,
the more I try to get victory in my prayer life, the more the number
of distractions seems to increase. Also, when I'm praying, I often get
a strong sense that I need to hurry in order to get on to something
else. Items on my "to do" list bombard my mind with such urgency
that being still and engaging the Lord—abiding in His presence—

is a huge challenge. Satan, the world, and the flesh work feverishly in concert to keep you and me preoccupied with worldly concerns instead of attentive to what the Spirit would lead us to pray about. We must find our refuge for prayer in the secret place that David described:

> He who dwells in the secret place of the Most High,
> Shall abide under the shadow of the Almighty.
> I will say of the LORD, "He is my refuge and my fortress;
> My God, in Him I will trust." (Psalm 91:1–2)

Jesus said it this way: "When you pray, go into your room, and when you have shut the door, pray to your Father who is in the secret place; and your Father who sees in secret will reward you openly" (Matthew 6:6). When Jesus said to "shut the door," He was telling us to shut out all distractions, including interference from the spiritual realm.

Evangelist, teacher, and writer Oswald Chambers confirmed that this isn't easy to do:

> Prayer is an effort of the will. After we have entered our secret place and shut the door, the most difficult thing to do is to pray. We cannot seem to get our minds into good working order, and the first thing we have to fight is wandering thoughts. The great battle in private prayer is overcoming this problem of our idle and wandering thinking. We have to learn to discipline our minds and concentrate on willful, deliberate prayer. Jesus says to "shut your door." Having a secret stillness before God means deliberately shutting the door on our emotions and remembering Him.[1]

A specific room where we can go each day and physically shut a door to pray might be helpful to some degree, but we would still have to fight "wandering thoughts" and make the effort to "discipline our minds." Clearly, the secret place is more than physical. The secret place is anywhere we can be still with the Lord, and that fact is very good news because we need constant connection to His presence. Wherever we are, we can—by God's grace—shut out the world, listen for our Lord to speak, and open our hearts to pray to our heavenly Father.

And, from cover to cover, the Bible gives us real-life examples of the power of such prayer. Basically, prayer is the means we use to communicate with God, but the potential of that simple conversation is unlimited. Prayer brings heaven to earth and earth to heaven. It is the bridge between the supernatural and the natural. Through prayer, God puts angels in motion and demons to flight. I once heard a sermon where pastor and author Craig Groeschel said, "Prayers prompted by the Holy Spirit are like extremely accurate missiles that can fly right down hell's smokestacks and demolish enemy strongholds." To get these kinds of results, however, we definitely need to "discipline our minds," as Oswald Chambers said.

PRAYER WARRIORS WHO HAVE GONE BEFORE US

We already know, from the book of Ephesians alone, that the apostle Paul was a prayer warrior; so let's consider the prayer life of a couple other mighty men of God and learn from them about communicating with the Father.

David was a mighty man of God who consistently sought his Lord's face in prayer. Despite his many failures, David loved God and turned to Him for guidance in almost every situation he faced in life. In fact, it is on record for all eternity that David was "a man after [God's] own heart" (1 Samuel 13:14). He wrote many of the psalms, and they are some of the greatest songs and prayers ever penned.

Take a few moments and read Psalm 18 to see the warrior-poet proclaiming his faith in his Warrior God and praising God for how He responded to his prayers for help. Or check out Psalm 5 where David cried out to the Lord for guidance and protection from his enemies. Pore over Psalm 51 where David plumbed the depths of despair in a prayer of heartfelt repentance over his fall into sin with Bathsheba—or, in sharp contrast, see David exuberantly praising God for His majesty and love in Psalm 145.

Holding nothing back, David passionately expressed all of his emotions and took all of his cares to the God he loved and trusted. David was in a beautiful love relationship with his Lord, and his prayers attest to that fact. Why do you and I not take time to seek God as wholeheartedly as David did? Or cry out to Him in our despair? Or thank Him in such detail for His love and faithfulness toward us?

Finally, what can we learn about prayer from Jesus Himself? Consider what the writer of Hebrews reported:

> During the days of Jesus' life on earth, he offered up prayers and petitions with fervent cries and tears to the one who could save him from death, and he was heard because of his reverent submission. (Hebrews 5:7 NIV)

Were you surprised by how that sentence ended? You'd think the reason Jesus' prayers were heard was because He was the only Son of God. Instead the verse says Jesus' prayers were heard "because of his reverent submission." Jesus—the King of kings and Lord of lords—chose to submit Himself to the Father's will, and He lived out His days on earth praying humbly and reverently. Jesus passionately poured out His heart to His Father with "cries and tears."

Scripture tells us Jesus prayed in the early morning hours (Mark 1:35), He prayed all through the night (Luke 6:12), He prayed in Gethsemane where He even asked His disciples to pray for Him (Mark 14:35–38), He prayed for His band of brothers (John 17:6–17), and He prayed for all of us believers (John 17:20–26). Jesus modeled for us a prayer life that pleased God. He fervently prayed. He petitioned. He cried out. He got His marching orders daily, and then He took action by preaching, teaching, healing, and serving people.

TRUTHS ABOUT PRAYER

In addition to learning about prayer from the examples of Paul, David, and Jesus, we can also learn from the New Testament letter of James. It contains some amazingly powerful promises concerning our prayer life. Consider, for instance, that in James 5:13–18 the writer used the words *pray* or *prayer* seven times. James ended the passage with these words:

> Elijah was a man with a nature like ours, and he prayed earnestly that it would not rain; and it did not rain on the land for three years and six months. And he prayed again, and the heaven gave rain, and the earth produced its fruit. (James 5:17–18)

James was referring to the time when Elijah prayed for rain in 1 Kings 18:41–46. There was a severe drought in the land, but God told Elijah rain was coming. So Elijah bowed down, prayed, and then asked his servant to go look out over the sea for rain. Nothing. So Elijah prayed some more and sent him again. Nothing. This goes on for—you might have guessed it—seven times.

Both passages emphasize the need for persistence in our prayer lives. It's also important to note that James said Elijah was "a man with a nature like ours" (James 5:17). He wasn't any different from you or me, but his faith and persistence make him an example for all future prayer warriors to follow: Never give up! Never lose heart!

After the seventh try, Elijah's servant saw a cloud "as small as a man's hand, rising out of the sea!" (1 Kings 18:44). Elijah knew it was God's answer: an abundance of rain was coming. But notice that the answer started out small. Don't despise small beginnings. Sometimes

God answers our prayers gradually as we continue to pray. Trust God that the cloudburst is coming!

James summed up the warrior prayer life with this: "The effective, fervent prayer of a righteous man avails much" (James 5:16). Our prayers matter to God, and they make a huge difference in the outcome of human affairs. If we truly want to join God in The Advance, one very effective way is to offer to God fervent, passionate prayers in the Spirit. When we don't know how to pray, the Bible tells us to press on, trusting that the Spirit will make our weak prayers effective:

> The Spirit also helps in our weaknesses. For we do not know what we should pray for as we ought, but the Spirit Himself makes intercession for us with groanings which cannot be uttered. Now He who searches the hearts knows what the mind of the Spirit is, because He makes intercession for the saints according to the will of God. (Romans 8:26–27)

Turn-of-the-twentieth-century pastor and writer Andrew Murray says in his book *The Prayer Life*, "It is nothing but the sin of prayerlessness, which is the cause of the lack of a powerful spiritual life!"[2] Prayerlessness is sin? When I read that, I was so convicted. I knew Murray was absolutely right. We were all created to make a difference for the Lord in this world, and God shows us over and over, in account after account of His faithful people, that prayer is key.

E. M. Bounds says:

> The soldiers in the warfare against the Devil must understand how to wear the armor of *"all prayer"* (Ephesians 6:18). The demand is for *"all prayer"* at all seasons, in the intensest form, with a deep sense of personal need for God. Prayer must deepen and intensify into supplication. The Holy Spirit will help us into this kind of mighty praying and clothe us with this irresistible power of prayer.[3]

Prayer is a crucial weapon—as well as a privilege, responsibility, and lifeline. The veil separating us from our pure and holy God in the temple's Most Holy Place was torn in two when Jesus died on the cross (Matthew 27:50–51). Now we can boldly enter the throne room of God with our cares and concerns 24/7. There, we can listen to the Spirit and pray God's will with confidence and faith, knowing our God is ready to respond. Praying in the Spirit, we can confront the spiritual forces of evil that are hindering us, our church, or those we love, and make them flee. There, also, we receive our marching orders, and God expects us to obey and take action. That's how Jesus did it. That's how Paul did it. It's the only way we can do it. This is war—so be a prayer warrior!

PAUL'S PRAYER REQUEST—AND OURS

I end our focus on Ephesians with Paul's own prayer request. Paul understood the power of prayer and therefore the necessity of having prayer warriors lifting him up. Only then could he boldly, clearly, and effectively advance the gospel. As we move forward in obedience to that same charge—the Great Commission of Matthew 28:18–20—we need the same prayer coverage. Surrounding yourself with prayer warriors is a prelude to victory.

> [Pray] for me, that utterance may be given to me, that I may open my mouth boldly to make known the mystery of the gospel, for which I am an ambassador in chains; that in it I may speak boldly, as I ought to speak. (Ephesians 6:19–20)

WAR ROOM DISCUSSION

1. Why do you personally struggle to pray? What might you do to overcome that obstacle and become more consistent, more focused, or more persistent?

2. Who in the Bible comes to mind when you hear the words *prayer warrior*? Why does that person inspire you? What aspect of his/her prayer life will you apply to your own?

3. Of the people you know or know of, who inspires you to pray? What does that person do that you will apply to your prayer life?

4. When you think of answered prayer in your own life, what one or two instances come to mind? Find encouragement in those examples of God's faithful responses to your heartfelt prayer.

5. In *The Prayer Life* Andrew Murray wrote, "It is nothing but the sin of prayerlessness, which is the cause of the lack of a powerful spiritual life." Do you agree or disagree? Why? And if you agree, what will be your response to this insight?

IO

EQUIPPED
READY FOR MY MISSION

WEAPONS OF OUR WARFARE

*Though we live in the world, we do not
wage war as the world does.
The weapons we fight with
are not the weapons of the world.*

2 CORINTHIANS 10:3-4 NIV

One day I was invited to go skeet shooting with a group of men from my church. Having handled a gun only one other time in my life, I was fired up (no pun intended) to get another shot at it (okay, pun intended). After we arrived at the cabin, my friends started taking a variety of firearms out of their cars, and—I must admit—I felt like a little boy among giants. As they started inspecting and loading their weaponry, I could tell all of them were quite comfortable, experienced, and proficient. I was a total novice in this world of guns and ammo—and I was anxious to learn all I could.

The day was an absolute blast (sorry, couldn't resist). I had so much fun missing clay targets that, afterward, I told Cindy I was going to buy a gun and become an expert myself. That's when I sensed the Lord say to me, "This is all great, but how much expertise do you have in wielding *spiritual* weapons?" I winced as my dull sword came to mind. Sure, a gun could be of some use to me, but spiritual weapons are crucial for God's people to survive the daily battles in life. If I am truly committed to being a spiritual warrior, why am I not excited about becoming an expert in spiritual weaponry?

God has given us mighty weapons for warfare, and He rightfully expects us to become highly skilled in using them. We master them not only for our own battles, but also in order to be able to train and equip fellow warriors. So what are the spiritual weapons we have available? I think anything we read about in the Bible that effectively disarms Satan can be considered a spiritual weapon. That being said, the list below is definitely not exhaustive; you may think of many other weapons. The important thing is to be thoroughly familiar with what you have in your arsenal. Soldiers in live combat have been trained to use all kinds of weapons, and in the heat of battle, they have to decide which weapon to use, which weapon will be most effective. Spiritual war is no different. So stockpile your arsenal, keep your skill with the various weapons sharp, and listen for the Spirit to guide.

OUR SPIRITUAL ARMORY

The Word of God (the sword of the Spirit): As we discussed in chapter 8, this sword is our mightiest weapon, and it is our duty to keep it sharp by daily reading God's Word. Remember, "the word of God is living and powerful, and sharper than any two-edged sword" (Hebrews 4:12). The Spirit will enable us to take out the Enemy by giving us the word (*logos*) to speak (*rhema*).

The Blood of Jesus: The power of Jesus' blood to overcome the Enemy is phenomenal. Satan assails us with accusations, but the blood of our Savior has acquitted us. Jesus took the "guilty" sentence and died, so He could declare us "not guilty." By Jesus' blood shed on the cross, we receive forgiveness (Matthew 26:28), a clear conscience (Hebrews 9:14), redemption (Ephesians 1:7), justification (Romans 5:9), confidence to enter the Most Holy Place (Hebrews10:19), and the list goes on. Pray the protection of Christ's blood daily over your family, your domain (your home, property, and possessions), and yourself (see Exodus 12:13).

Also, in battle, pinpoint your target when you pray. If you are feeling condemned, say, "In the authority given to me and by the shed blood of Jesus Christ, I come against all condemning spirits and cast them away from me in Jesus' name." Name whatever it is that is coming against you and then claim the powerful blood of Jesus as your protection and shield. Even if you have given Satan a foothold through your sin, repent and proclaim aloud that the blood of your Savior has cleansed you of all sin and defuses all of Satan's lies and accusations. Revelation 12:11 says that we overcome Satan "by the blood of the Lamb and by the word of [our] testimony." Derek Prince said, "Testify personally to what the Word of God says that the blood of Jesus does for you." Whether you speak the verses listed in the preceding paragraph or find others, boldly declare the truths about the power of Jesus' blood.

The Name of Jesus: The very name of our Savior and Lord strikes fear and dread into Satan and his army, and that is why the name of Jesus is such a powerful weapon. Satan and his army fear no other being and no other name; they only fear Jesus. They don't fear you, but they fear Jesus *in* you, and they understand the authority you are granted in His name.

Consider what the name of Jesus has and will accomplish: every knee will bow (Philippians 2:10), the lame are healed (Acts 3:6), demons are cast out (Mark 16:17), faith in His name brings "perfect soundness" (Acts 3:16), and sin is forgiven (1 John 2:12). Jesus said, "Whatever you ask in my name, that I will do" (John 14:13–14). Letting the name of Jesus be a weapon in battle does not mean just tacking His name onto the end of a prayer. Jesus' name commands authority, and we are blessed to walk by faith in His delegated authority, knowing we wield great power when we invoke His name into our circumstances.

Prayer: Prayer is the vital link to a deeper, more meaningful relationship with our heavenly Father. This deeper Father-son connection will, in turn, result in greater and greater victories for His kingdom as we learn to pray power-filled, God-willed prayers of faith. Clinton E. Arnold made this observation: "In Ephesians 6:18–20, prayer is seen as essential to the arming of believers with the power of God .... the writer (Paul) thus wants his readers to understand prayer as an essential spiritual weapon, but more than a weapon. It is foundational for the deployment of all the other weapons."[1]

Humility: From birth to death, Jesus' life on this earth was a picture of humility, and by His humble submission to the Father's will, He "[destroyed] the works of the devil" (1 John 3:8). Our Lord succeeded in His assignment to destroy the power of sin and death because He totally surrendered Himself to God's plan, and Jesus' surrender included laying down His life for us.

Like our Savior, when we humbly submit to God, we are saying *no* to pride and self-rule and *yes* to God and His mission for our lives. It sounds counterintuitive, but to achieve victory in this war against Satan, we must surrender to God. We can't stand strong against our Enemy until we kneel before our Savior. We must love God with all of our heart and live in total dependence on Him.

> Dr. Ed Murphy put it this way: "'Submit therefore to God' [James 4:7] implies a surrender to the lordship of Christ. It is a total commitment of the whole person and each individual area of the life to the lordship of God. Without doubt, this surrender to God is the principle key to victory in spiritual warfare."[2]

Be a humble warrior, and God will give you favor and exalt you above your enemies (1 Peter 5:5–6).

Love: We who put our faith in God are filled to overflowing with His unlimited, unconditional love. Not only does His love flow through us to bless others, but His love is also a mighty weapon against the forces of evil. Romans 12:21 says, "Don't let evil conquer you, but conquer evil by doing good" (NLT). Loving and serving others—including and maybe especially our enemies—will undo works of darkness and help set free those people held captive by lies, pain, purposelessness, and many other chains. Remember, God is love and we are His ambassadors on the Earth, commissioned to share that love as well as the gospel account of its source.

Walking in the Power and Gifts of the Holy Spirit: The gifts of the Spirit are as necessary today as they were in the early church. God desires the Spirit to be alive and active in us as individual believers and in our church body corporately. Be willing for the Spirit to work in you and through you. So if you haven't before, spend time exploring the gifts God has given you and praying for the ways He would have you use them—in the power of the Spirit—to serve and build up the body of Christ. This is the way the apostle Paul put it: "Since you are eager for gifts of the Spirit, try to excel in those that build up the church" (1 Corinthians 14:12 NIV).

Fasting: Spiritual fasting is a time of denying our flesh its physical needs and letting our physical hunger help us focus on spiritual hunger for God. Fasting clears the way for us to hear and connect to Him unhindered. Also, some Enemy strongholds are so fortified they can only be demolished by faith, prayer, and fasting. Jesus didn't say, "If you fast...," wording that would have made the discipline optional. Instead Jesus said—and He said it twice—"When you fast" (Matthew 6:16–17). Denying ourselves is to be a regular part of our life and our walk in the Spirit. So when the battle heats up, fast and pray.

Praise and Worship: We talked about the power of worship in warfare in chapter 7. The Enemy hates our praise to God, so keep a song of praise in your heart. Sing it often and, yes, sing it aloud. God will be pleased, and the demons will run and flee. Praise silences the Enemy:

> Through the praise of children and infants you have established a stronghold against your enemies, to silence the foe and the avenger. (Psalm 8:2 NIV)

DEMOLISHING ENEMY STRONGHOLDS

*The weapons we fight with... have divine power to demolish
strongholds. We demolish arguments and every pretension
that sets itself up against the knowledge of God, and we
take captive every thought to make it obedient to Christ.*

2 CORINTHIANS 10:4–5 NIV

Now that we have an arsenal of mighty weapons we can employ in our
daily battles, we can use them to free ourselves and others from spiritual
bondage and the Enemy's strongholds. As I stated earlier, a stronghold
is a place of personal bondage built on a lie or deception that the Enemy
has been able to establish in our minds because we either didn't know
God's truth or haven't trusted in it. I highly recommend reading Neil T.
Anderson's book *Victory Over the Darkness*. In it he wrote:

> A stronghold is a mental habit pattern. It is memory traces
> burned into our minds over time or by the intensity of traumatic
> experiences. For instance, inferiority is a stronghold. Nobody
> is born inferior to anyone else, but you could be struggling
> with an inferiority complex if you kept getting the message
> from the world that everyone is stronger, smarter and [better
> looking] than you.[3]

Anderson goes on to say, "Satan's strategy is to introduce his thoughts and
ideas into your mind and deceive you into believing they are yours.... If
Satan can place a thought in your mind—and he can—it isn't much of a
trick for him to make you think it is your idea."[4] In his book *The Three
Battlegrounds* Francis Frangipane agrees: "Wherever a stronghold exists,
it is a demonically induced pattern of thinking. Specifically, it is a 'house
made of thoughts' which has become a dwelling place for satanic activity."[5]

In 2 Corinthians 10:4–5, the *arguments* Paul mentioned are
schemes and deceptive thoughts the Enemy uses to bring us into

bondage. *Pretensions* have to do with pride and relying on ourselves instead of God. The Enemy uses these arguments and pretensions to ensnare us in a pattern of faulty thinking. The longer we have been enslaved to the lie or confused belief, the more fortified the stronghold. It is by surrendering to Christ, being filled with His presence, and knowing and speaking His Word with authority that we will demolish our strongholds. Francis Frangipane continues: "It is the presence of the Lord coming forth in us that makes the weapons of our warfare mighty, empowering our words with authority as we pull down strongholds."

Strongholds are formed in our minds, but Paul taught that we can "take captive every thought to make it obedient to Christ" (2 Corinthians 10:5 NIV). But are you and I regularly examining our thoughts to see if they align with God's truth? Making thoughts obedient to Christ means examining the thought before we let it settle in our minds, start dwelling on it, and come into agreement with it. Is the thought in compliance with what God's Word says? Does it fall within the parameters of healthy Christian thinking as in Philippians 4:8? Specifically, is it true, noble, just, pure, lovely, of good report, virtuous, or praiseworthy? Or are we being held captive to the lies we've let take root?

The Enemy may have ensnared you with a lie like *You just don't measure up* or *You will never be good enough.* The Enemy himself may have sown that seed in your mind, or he may have had someone speak that lie directly to you. Either way, if you weren't aware of what God's Word says about you, you had no defense against Satan's lie about your worth. If we come into agreement with the lie, Satan will then tempt us to deal with the wound and/or ease the pain it causes by numbing ourselves with alcohol, drugs, food, sex, tobacco, television, etc. Or maybe you are dealing with emotional strongholds such as pride, worry, fear, anger, depression, bitterness, jealousy, or rebellion. Whatever the case, if we are struggling to overcome an addiction or negative emotion, we may be dealing with a demonic stronghold. That is simply a spiritual reality. Remember, you are at war!

TAKING THE HIGH GROUND

When I think of Enemy strongholds, the opening scene of *Saving Private Ryan* comes to mind. Though brutal to watch, it serves as a great analogy for dealing with strongholds. The Germans were entrenched in fortified strongholds in the high cliffs above Omaha Beach when the American landing crafts arrived. For hours our soldiers were pinned down by enemy fire. The enemy had the high ground, and until those strongholds were taken out, our men would keep losing the battle, and many would die. Committed warriors, our men courageously kept advancing, and when they eventually destroyed the strongholds, they found that the enemy forces were much thinner on the other side. At that point our men successfully completed their mission with much less resistance. The reason? The strongholds had been broken.[6]

The same holds true for us in our war against our spiritual Enemy. We give Satan and his armies the advantage when we fall into sin or agree with his lies. When that happens, we must come humbly before God and repent. Then, putting on our armor, taking up our sword, raising our shields, and getting back into the fight, we seize the victory that Christ has already won for us.

Consider these verses from Jeremiah and the great wisdom they offer for dealing with Enemy strongholds:

> The LORD put forth His hand and touched my
> mouth, and the LORD said to me:
>> "Behold, I have put My words in your mouth.
>> See, I have this day set you over the nations
>>> and over the kingdoms,
>> To root out and to pull down,
>> To destroy and to throw down,
>> To build and to plant." (Jeremiah 1:9–10)

God put His all-powerful Word in Jeremiah's mouth and then "set [him] over" (remember that we are seated with Christ in a position of victory) nations and kingdoms, two symbols of strongholds of evil. God then revealed His Word's power to root out, pull down, and destroy kingdoms (in our case, the kingdom of darkness) when we speak aloud God's truth with faith. That is exactly what we have to do to our strongholds: root them out, pull them down, and destroy them with God's Word.

Conversely, God revealed at the end of Jeremiah 1:10 that speaking His Word also has the power to build us back up and firmly establish us (*plant*). In His resurrected Son, God has given us both the high ground and the ammunition we need to annihilate strongholds and be free to serve Him.

REVEAL, RENOUNCE, REPENT, REPLACE

Below are four practical steps you can take to demolish demonic strongholds. But first, enter into God's presence by praising Him for who He is.... Thank Him for the many blessings He showers on you and for the promises He makes and keeps.... Then—asking the Holy Spirit to lead you—pray through the process of Reveal, Renounce, Repent, and Replace.

1. **Reveal** *Root Out*: Satan is looking for opportunities to establish and maintain his strongholds, so we need to make sure we aren't helping him do that. As you pray, ask the Holy Spirit to reveal the intel you need. I am amazed that every time I go through this process, the Spirit brings to mind additional wounds that I need Jesus to heal and/or another sin or wrong way of thinking that is hindering my walk with God. Get a pen and a pad of paper and write down anything He brings to mind as you go through this process:

   • We all struggle with pride, and this is the first stronghold that must come down. So humbly admit to God how badly you need His presence and His power to pull down the strongholds in your life. In particular, ask forgiveness for the sins of pride and self-reliance.

- Ask the Spirit to reveal any sin in your past that may still be impeding your Christian growth today.

- Ask Him to call to mind any people in your life who have wounded or offended you but whom you haven't completely forgiven. (Forgiveness can be difficult, but when I am struggling to forgive someone, I always remind myself of Christ's generous and ongoing forgiveness of me.)

- Have you had any involvement in occult practices—with Ouija boards, séances, astrology/horoscopes, fortune-tellers, tarot cards, playing occult-type computer games, etc.—that may have opened the door to demonic influence in your life? Confess those—and stop those activities if you haven't already.

- Ask the Lord to reveal any of the Deceiver's lies you have believed and help you recognize crippling words others have spoken to you. It may be an emotional wound from your childhood that you've repressed. Maybe, for instance, someone said to you, "You are worthless" or "You will never amount to anything." Or maybe your thinking about God is based more on how your parent(s) treated you than on what the Bible teaches about Him. In other words, do you see God as a cruel taskmaster just waiting to scold you and reject you when you do wrong, or do you see Him as a loving Father who is always looking out for your best interest? The former view leads to bondage; the latter, to freedom. Jesus said, "The truth will set you free!" (John 8:32).

- Last, what do you believe about yourself? How do you feel about yourself? Do you understand who you are in Christ and the incredible inheritance and mission you have received as a son of the King? (Review the warrior declarations at the end of chapter 3, "Delivered").

2. **Renounce** *Pull Down*: Now renounce any sin and every lie that the Holy Spirit revealed to you. Renounce each one and break agreement with them. For example, in prayer say, "I renounce the lie that *I am worthless*, and I break all agreement with that lie—right now—in Jesus' name." Repeat this kind of renunciation for every sin or lie the Spirit brought to mind.

3. **Repent** *Pull Down*: Now ask God to forgive you for any specific sin or lie the Spirit revealed to you. Perhaps you need to repent of sin (anger, lust, idolatry, resentment, bitterness, etc.). Tell God you agree with Him that what you did, said, or thought was sinful. Then, repent (which means to turn from the sin and go in the opposite direction). Finally, ask God to cleanse you of your sin—and that's what Jesus' blood makes possible.

4. **Replace** *Destroy, Build Up, Plant*: Replace the lies you have believed with God's truth that you speak aloud. This step is essential! Find verses that reinforce what God says about you and the particular area of bondage you're dealing with. Then, right under the lies you wrote down, list several truths from God's Word that address the stronghold you've been dealing with. Then pray those specific truths and promises. As you fill your mind daily and speak aloud God's powerful Word, you will take away the power of Satan's lies, and you will more readily recognize his deception when you hear it. Then you can take those thoughts captive when you first hear them.

In Romans 12:2, Paul put it this way: "Do not be conformed to the pattern of this world, but be transformed by the renewing of your mind." Prayer and meditating on specific Bible verses will help you renew your mind and keep it filled with God's truth rather than Satan's lies. Pray this prayer or something like it:

Lord, I thank You for revealing to me these areas of bondage in my life. I ask Your forgiveness for [name the particular sin], and I humbly repent of this sin. I also confess that I have believed Satan's lies and not trusted in Your Word. I renounce [name the sin or lie], and I break all agreement with it right now. I bring the truth of Your Word against Satan's lies, and I choose to trust in Your promises that say [speak particular verses]. Lord, You disarmed Satan at the cross (Colossians 2:15), and I bring the power of Your Cross and Your blood against him right now. I ask that You break any and all demonic influence over my life and that You will help me walk closely with You.

Thank You that no weapon formed against me shall prosper and that I can refute every tongue that rises against me (Isaiah 54:17). Thank You that Your blood cleanses me from all sin (1 John 1:7) and that when I confess my sin, You are faithful and just to forgive me and purify me from all unrighteousness (1 John 1:9). I thank You that I am no longer in bondage to Satan and his lies and that I will continue to overcome him by the blood of the Lamb and the Word of my testimony (Revelation 12:11). I loose freedom, peace, and healing in my soul, and I stand strong in You and in Your mighty power (Ephesians 6:10). I pray all of this according to Your holy Word and by the authority given to me by the shed blood of Jesus Christ. Amen.

Sometimes we will have to endure hardship for a while before our breakthrough comes, but don't lose heart. Victory *is* guaranteed, and it will come in God's timing. I love David's perspective on the value of hardship: "It is good for me that I have been afflicted, that I might learn Your statutes" (Psalm 119:71). Learn God's statutes and keep blasting that bunker with a barrage of Scripture until the stronghold is nothing but smoldering ashes. Victory is assured in God's Word, so thank Him that the victory over your strongholds is already won in the heavenly realms.

GET IN THE FIGHT

Now that the eyes of your heart have been opened to this spiritual war as well as to the weapons you have available, I challenge you to read the Bible from the perspective of a soldier. With your new intel and insight, I believe you will see the entirety of Scripture in a new way: you will read it as a warrior called to fight the good fight in an epic battle to advance God's kingdom. And I believe you will find in Scripture, as you open it daily, new intel and ammunition for your arsenal.

> I have pursued my enemies and overtaken them;
> Neither did I turn my back again till they were destroyed.
> I have wounded them,
> So that they could not rise;
> They have fallen under my feet.
> For You have armed me with strength for the battle;
> You have subdued under me those who rose up against me.
> You have also given me the necks of my enemies,
> So that I destroyed those who hated me.
> They cried out, but there was none to save;
> Even to the LORD, but He did not answer them.
> Then I beat them as fine as the dust before the wind;
> I cast them out like dirt in the streets. (Psalm 18:37–42)

David went to war and didn't let up until his enemies were dust under his feet, and then he rejoiced in his victory. You can do the same. Follow David's example. Be a warrior for the Almighty! Get on your knees, put on your armor, and get in the fight today. Right now!

Proclaim your allegiance to Christ and praise Him for who you are in Him!

Believe that you, Warrior, are more than a conqueror!

Say it with me, "I am a warrior!"

WAR ROOM DISCUSSION

1. Which of the weapons listed—if any—surprised you? Why? Which weapon(s) do you want to be more skilled in using? What will you do to reach that goal?

2. What burdensome thoughts and ideas of your own might actually have been introduced by the Evil One? Think, for instance, about words and phrases that are a regular part of your self-talk even though they beat you up and wear you down.

3. What biblical truths about your identity, your value, God's love, or any of a number of topics will you choose to memorize so that you can destroy the lies that echo around in your mind and heart?

4. Reveal, Renounce, Repent, Replace: Comment on the wisdom of this progression. What value did working through these steps have for you—or what do you expect God to do through these four steps when you do work through them?

5. Finally, in three or four sentences, proclaim your allegiance to Christ and/or write your own warrior's prayer.

EPILOGUE

You will show me the path of life;
in your presence is fullness of joy.
PSALM 16:11

The path of life leads upward for the wise.
PROVERBS 15:24 NIV

There comes a time when we must forsake all fear and get serious about becoming the mighty warriors God created us to be. We will do so for the sake of our King, His kingdom, and the people we love. That time is now, for the hour is late, and warriors are in great demand. Will you step up?

In the book of Ephesians, God has taught us much about the battle and how He has prepared us to fight and defeat our Enemy. I pray you are ready to stand, walk, and war in the spiritual realm, to step into the victory that God has secured. I pray that you are confident about whom you belong to and therefore confident about who you are. Know, too, that God will guide your steps as—in faith, in prayer—you look to Him for direction. After all, it's His path and His plan for us who have been raised up and seated with Christ. Our King has given us full authority to carry out our mission. God has promised us the land and equipped us for the battle. But, remember, we are invading Enemy territory, so we must humbly listen for God's voice, obey Him, stand strong in His truth, and take back the land His way—and His way is by faith.

I am not recommending it, but the movie *Apocalypto* offered me a powerful lesson about facing my enemies. Toward the end of the movie, Jaguar Paw has been running for miles through the jungle, fleeing savage enemies. Once he realizes he is back on his home turf, he stops, and the camera zooms in. Jaguar Paw is remembering who he is and where he is. His warrior spirit rising, he declares, "This is my land." Then he turns around to face his enemies—and he fights back! His running-away days are over.

That is where we are, warrior. We don't need to run away from the Enemy. Yes, this is Enemy-occupied territory, and we are just passing through. Our citizenship is in heaven, but we have work to do here. We have battles to fight! By God's grace, our weapons of war have supernatural power, and we have complete authority to use them. So let's ask God to increase our faith, fill us with His Spirit, and enable us to take back the spiritual ground we have given up. Remember, Jesus has already defeated Satan!

Maybe the greatest news for our battle, though, is another mystery that Paul revealed: "This is the secret: Christ lives in you" (Colossians 1:27 NLT). Jesus died not only to reconcile you with God, but also to make His home within you. He will be there with you on the warrior's path every step of the way. Every morning you wake and whatever battle you face, Christ is in you.

Finally, you are called to fight for those people whom God places in your circle of influence and along your path in life. After all, He equips His warriors to serve others, not themselves. Many people all around us need to be rescued, and God is calling you and me to help set them free. I used to think that the passage below pertained only to the saints the writer had just listed. But one day the Lord pointed out to me that these verses apply to every generation. May these words be true of every warrior who serves God's kingdom:

> By faith, these people overthrew kingdoms, ruled with justice, and received what God had promised them. They shut the mouths of lions, quenched the flames of fire, and escaped death by the edge of the sword. Their weakness was turned to strength. They became strong in battle and put whole armies to flight. (Hebrews 11:33–34 NLT)

The path lies before you, and a grand adventure is waiting. You, mighty warrior of God, are fully equipped for your mission as part of the powerful army God is raising up.

So hear the promise the Lord of heaven's armies gave to the church in Ephesus:

> To him who overcomes I will give to eat from the tree of life,
> which is in the midst of the Paradise of God. (Revelation 2:7)

You are on the winning side! Keep fighting in God's strength, according to His leading, and with the weapons He has provided. And if I don't see you in this life, I will see you at the tree of life—in the Paradise of God!

THE WARRIOR'S ADVANCE PRAYER

Here is a recap of the prayers from the end of the chapters (Day One and the end of Day Seven are additions). Pray through a section each day over the next seven days to help establish your feet firmly on the warrior path.

Day One

Holy and awesome God,

I praise You today for Your greatness! You alone are greatly to be praised, and I will bless Your name forever. You are God Almighty, the Great I AM, the Ancient of Days, worthy of all my praise and worship for who You are and for what You've done. I love You with all my heart, soul, mind, and strength, and I come humbly before You now to honor You as my King and my Sovereign Lord. I offer my body to You as a living sacrifice. I consecrate my heart and this time of prayer to You completely, surrendering my life and choosing to be totally dependent on You.

Thank You for the incredible warrior path You have revealed to me in Your holy Word. Thank You, also, for authoring my story and including me in Your glorious plan. Help me to courageously stand, walk, and war on the warrior path in the power of Your Spirit. Conform me, throughout this day, to be more and more like Christ my King. Train me well and mold me into a good soldier, equipped to fight the good fight for Your glorious kingdom.

Day Two

Ephesians 1: Stand

Father, I take my stand on all of Your promises today. Thank You for rescuing me, redeeming me, and placing me in Christ. Through Him I receive every spiritual blessing that You bestow. I also thank You that I am saved, redeemed, chosen, holy, blameless, an adopted son, accepted, forgiven, predestined for Your mission, and sealed by the Holy Spirit. I pray for Your wisdom and revelation and ask that You would open my spiritual eyes and enable me to live in the hope of Your calling. I fully receive the glorious inheritance I have in You as an adopted son. Fill me, this day, with Your incredible resurrection power that You graciously make available to me by Your Spirit. In Jesus' powerful name I pray. Amen.

Day Three
Ephesians 2: Stand

Heavenly Father, thank You for the cross, for Your victory over sin and death, for raising me from the dead and giving me new life in Christ. I am crucified with Christ, and I no longer live but Christ lives in me. I renounce all agreements I have made with the world, my flesh, and the Enemy. Empower me by Your Spirit to overcome these enemies of my soul. Thank You for seating me with Christ in a position of victory and for Your precious blood that has reconciled me to You and allows me to walk in Your peace. Jesus, I pray the protective covering of Your blood over my family, my home, and all of my domain today. You alone are the Cornerstone of my faith and the Rock on which I stand. I surrender my life to You today, for Your purposes and glory. In Jesus' name I pray. Amen.

Day Four
Ephesians 3: Stand

Father, You have given all authority, power, dominion, and rule to Your Holy Son, Jesus. I humbly thank You for sharing that authority and power with me. Increase my belief in this truth, so I can be effective for Your kingdom today. Thank You, also, for revealing the mystery of Your incredible plan to me. I am blessed to be a part of Your powerful body, the church, and I pray for my local church as well as for the worldwide body of believers: raise us up together as a mighty army for You and for the advancement of Your kingdom. By Your Spirit strengthen me with power, love, and a sound mind. Help me to fully receive the extravagant love You have for me and to show that love to the people You place in my path today. In Jesus' name I pray. Amen.

Day Five
Ephesians 4: Walk

Father, I ask You to empower me to walk boldly in Your Spirit as I follow You. Help me to promote unity in the body. Strengthen me to walk worthy of my calling as Your son and a warrior in Your army. I pray for closer connections with Your people. Help me also to establish and maintain a close brotherhood of men to fight the battle with. Reveal to me the gifts You have blessed me with and help me use them so I am a blessing to those around me. I put off all my former conduct as the old man and put on the Lord Jesus Christ to walk as the new man today. I commit to stand strong in the Warrior Code of Ethics and dare to be different so people will see that difference and know that I live for You. May my life bring You glory. In Jesus' name I pray. Amen.

Day Six
Ephesians 5: Walk

Heavenly Father, I ask You to conform me more and more into the image of Christ today as I live to imitate Him. I pray that, by Your Spirit, I will walk in more power, love, light, and wisdom than ever before. Fill me with all the fullness of Your love, so I can pour it out to those I encounter today. Give me ears to hear Your voice as I walk the path in the light of Your presence. Remind me to live with a mind-set of worship and stay close to You today, filled with Your abundant life. I surrender my home, my marriage, my family, and myself to You. Lead me and teach me to be a better husband and father. Show me creative ways to bless and cherish my wife, and I thank You for making us heirs together of the grace of life. In Jesus' powerful name I pray. Amen.

Day Seven
Ephesians 6: War

Lord, thank You for equipping me for spiritual battle with each piece of Your armor. I strap on the belt of truth and stand on Your Word that protects me from all the lies and deception of the Evil One. I put on the breastplate of righteousness that guards my heart from condemnation and shame. I stand strong in the shoes of peace that give me confidence to move forward and advance the Gospel. I take up the shield of faith that defuses all of Satan's fiery arrows. I put on the helmet of salvation and receive the mind of Christ so I can clearly hear Your voice and walk in step with You. Give me a renewed love and passion for Your Word and, in the heat of battle, may it be a sharp sword coming forth from my mouth by the guidance of the Holy Spirit.

Lord, thank You for creating me to be a warrior in Your army. Help me to stand strong and courageous for You. Give me faith that can move mountains. Fill me with Your love and compassion that, as You did, I might serve and lay down my life for Your people. Help me to be still, to hear Your voice, and to go where You send me. Empower me by Your Spirit to be a world changer and to live with abandon for You. Thank You for listening to and answering my prayers. I love You and give You all praise and honor for who You are, and who I am in You—a warrior with a cause, Your cause. And Yours is the kingdom and the power and the glory forever. In Jesus' incomparable name I pray. Amen.

ABOUT THE AUTHOR

Doug Smith enjoyed a sixteen-year career at Thomas Nelson Publishers in Nashville, Tennessee. In 2014 he began to pursue his dream of writing a book that would inspire men to live as warriors for Christ. He is a Christ-follower, worship leader, men's small-group leader, singer, songwriter, husband, and father. Doug currently serves on the worship team at Connect Church in Mount Juliet, Tennessee, where he and his wife, Cindy, live.

ACKNOWLEDGMENTS

I want to express my deepest thanks to all those who have encouraged me along the way on this journey. I had no idea what I was getting into, and your prayers and support were vital.

Cindy, you are my best friend and the love of my life. Thank you for always believing in me.

Lisa Guest, you were an answer to much prayer. Your skill and wisdom took this book to another level.

Allen Arnold, it's amazing how a man I barely know could have such a huge impact on this book coming to fruition. Thank you for the invitation—and the encouragement.

Lisa Stilwell, many thanks for all your great help and advice.

My band of brothers, my family, and my church family at Connect Church, I love you all.

ENDNOTES

Chapter 1

1 James Strong, *The New Strong's Expanded Exhaustive Concordance of the Bible Hebrew and Aramaic Dictionary* (Nashville, TN: Thomas Nelson, 1990), 292.
2 E. M. Bounds, *Guide to Spiritual Warfare* (New Kensington, PA: Whitaker House, 1984), 13.
3 Charles Stanley, *Overcoming the Enemy* (Nashville, TN: Thomas Nelson, 1997), 13, 14.

Chapter 2

1 Merriam-Webster Online Dictionary.
2 James Strong, *The New Strong's Expanded Dictionary of the Words in the Greek New Testament* (Nashville, TN: Thomas Nelson, 1990), 235.
3 Ibid.
4 Thayer's Greek Lexicon, Electronic Database. Copyright 2002, 2003, 2006, 2011 by Biblesoft, Inc.

Chapter 3

1 James Strong, *The New Strong's Expanded Dictionary of the Words in the Greek New Testament* (Nashville, TN: Thomas Nelson, 1990), 87.
2 John Eldredge, *Waking the Dead* (Nashville, TN: Thomas Nelson, 2003), 34.

Chapter 4

1 The NAS New Testament Greek Lexicon – biblestudytools.com.
2 *New Spirit-Filled Life Bible* (Nashville, TN: Thomas Nelson, 2002), 1625.
3 Charles Stanley, *Overcoming the Enemy* (Nashville, TN: Thomas Nelson, 1997), 69.

Chapter 5

1 Merriam-Webster Online Dictionary.
2 Mark Batterson, *Draw the Circle* (Grand Rapids, MI: Zondervan, 2012), 84.

Chapter 6

1 Merriam-Webster Online Dictionary
2 James Strong, *The New Strong's Expanded Dictionary of the Words in the Greek New Testament* (Nashville, TN: Thomas Nelson, 1990), 31.
3 Andrew Murray, *Humility* (London: James Nisbet & Co., 1896), 44.
4 Gordon Dalbey, *Healing the Masculine Soul* (Nashville, TN: W Publishing Group, a Division of Thomas Nelson Inc. 1988, 2003), xix.
5 Thayer's Greek Lexicon, Electronic Database. Copyright © 2002, 2003, 2006, 2011 by Biblesoft, Inc.

Chapter 7

1   John Eldredge, *Waking the Dead* (Nashville, TN: Thomas Nelson, 2003), 95.
2   James Strong, *The New Strong's Expanded Exhaustive Concordance of the Bible Hebrew and Aramaic Dictionary* (Nashville, TN: Thomas Nelson, 1990), 87.
3   Ibid.
4   Brown-Driver-Briggs Hebrew and English Lexicon, Unabridged, Electronic Database. Copyright © 2002, 2003, 2006 by Biblesoft, Inc.
5   James Strong, *The New Strong's Expanded Dictionary of the Words in the Greek New Testament* (Nashville, TN: Thomas Nelson, 1990), 230, 231.

Chapter 8

1   A. W. Tozer, Reclaiming Christianity (Ventura, California: Regal, 2009), 129.
2   Merriam-Webster Online Dictionary.
3   James Strong, *The New Strong's Expanded Dictionary of the Words in the Greek New Testament* (Nashville, TN: Thomas Nelson, 1990), 43.
4   Ibid., 92.
5   Ibid., 143, 144.
6   Ibid., 207.
7   Ibid., 202.
8   Ibid., 219.
9   Chip Ingram, *The Invisible War* (Grand Rapids, MI: Baker Books, 2006), 124.
10 Strong, 162.
11 Strong, 20.
12 Strong, 221.

Chapter 9

1   Oswald Chambers, *My Utmost For His Highest* (Uhrichsville, OH: Barbour Publishing, Inc.), August 23.
2   Andrew Murray, *The Prayer Life* (Chicago, IL: Moody Publishers 1941).
3   E. M. Bounds, *Guide to Spiritual Warfare* (New Kensington, PA: Whitaker House, 1984), 151.

Chapter 10

1   Clinton E. Arnold, *Power and Magic: The Concept of Power in Ephesians* (Cambridge: Cambridge University Press, 1989), 112.
2   Dr. Ed Murphy, *The Handbook for Spiritual Warfare* (Nashville, TN: Thomas Nelson Inc, 1992, 1996, 2003), 202.
3   Neil T. Anderson, *Victory Over the Darkness* (Ventura, CA: Regal Books, 2000), 157.
4   Ibid., 159, 160.
5   Francis Frangipane *An In-Depth View of the Three Arenas of Spiritual Warfare: The Mind, the Church and the Heavenly Places* (Cedar Rapids, IA: Arrow Publications, Inc., 2006), 33, 38.
6   John Eldredge *Wild at Heart* (Nashville, TN: Thomas Nelson, 2001, 2010), 87–90. John Eldredge uses the Normandy Beach landing to illustrate how a man's heart wounds can paralyze him with fear.